D0952240

HOW LIFE IMITATES CHESS

HOW LIFE IMITATES CHESS

MAKING THE RIGHT MOVES,
FROM THE BOARD TO THE BOARDROOM

GARRY KASPAROV

with Mig Greengard

BLOOMSBURY

Published by Bloomsbury USA, New York
Distributed to the trade by Holtzbrinck Publishers

All papers used by Bloomsbury USA are natural, recyclable products made from wood grown in well-managed forests. The manufacturing processes conform to the environmental regulations of the country of origin.

LIBRARY OF CONGRESS CATALOGING-IN-PUBLICATION DATA

Kasparov, G. K. (Garri Kimovich)
How life imitates chess : making the right moves, from the board to the boardroom / Garry Kasparov.—1st U.S. ed.
        p.   cm.
"October 2007."
ISBN-13: 978-1-59691-387-5
ISBN-10: 1-59691-387-8
1. Kasparov, G. K. (Garri Kimovich)   2. Chess players—Soviet Union—Biography.   3. Chess.
4. Decision making.   5. Strategy.   I. Title.

GV1439.K38A3   2007
794.1092—dc22
[B]
2007019706

First U.S. Edition 2007

1 3 5 7 9 10 8 6 4 2

Designed by Sara Stemen
Typeset by Westchester Book Group
Printed in the United States of America by Quebecor World Fairfield

To my mother, for a lifetime of inspiration and support.

CONTENTS

PART III

CONTENTS

OPENING GAMBIT

The Secret of Success

I was a teenage chess star in the chess-mad Soviet Union and became used to interviews and public speaking at a young age. Apart from occasional questions about hobbies and girls, these early interviews focused solely on my chess career. Then in 1985 I became the youngest world champion at the age of twenty-two, and from then on the type of questions I received changed dramatically. Instead of wanting to know about games and tournaments, people wanted to know how I had achieved my unprecedented success. How did I come to work so hard? How many moves ahead did I see? What went on in my mind during a game? Did I have a photographic memory? What did I eat? What did I do every night before going to sleep? In short, what were the secrets of my success?

It didn't take long for me to realize that I was disappointing my audiences with my answers. I worked hard because my mother taught me to. How many moves ahead I saw depended on the position. During a game I tried to recall my preparation and to calculate variations. My memory was good, but not photographic. I usually ate a heavy lunch of smoked salmon, steak, and tonic water before each game. (Sadly, when I hit my late thirties, my physical trainer put an end to this "diet.") Every night before going to bed I brushed my teeth. Not exactly inspiring material.

Everyone seemed to be looking for a precise method, a universal recipe people could follow to achieve great results every time. Famous writers are asked about what type of paper and pen they use, as if their tools are responsible for their writing. Such questions of course miss the point that we are all one of a kind, the result of millions of elements and transformations running from our DNA to this afternoon. We each build our own unique formula for making decisions, and every day we strive to make the best of this formula: to identify it, evaluate its performance, and find ways to improve it.

This book describes how my own formula developed, and how many people contributed to that development, directly and indirectly. The inspirational games of Alexander Alekhine, my first chess hero, find a place alongside the inspirational character of Winston Churchill, whose words and books I still turn to regularly. My parents—especially my mother—play an incalculable role, as do my teachers.

The idea for this book came when I realized that instead of coming up with clever answers for the eternal "What's going on in your head?" questions, it would be more interesting for me to actually find out. But the life of a chess professional, with its rigorous calendar of travel, play, and preparation, did not allow me much time for philosophical—as opposed to practical—introspection. When I retired from chess in March 2005, I finally gained the time and perspective to look back on my experiences and can now, finally, share them in a useful way.

This would be a very different book had I completed it before my dramatic career shift from chess to politics. First, I needed time to absorb the lessons that my life in chess had taught me. Second, my new experiences as a coalition leader, political organizer, and the public face of an opposition movement are forcing me to look at who I am and what I am capable of. Being passionate about advocating for democracy isn't enough. To build alliances and organize conferences requires me to apply my strategic vision and other chess skills in entirely new ways. After twenty-five years in a comfort zone of expertise, I stepped back and began to analyze my abilities so I could build and rebuild myself for these new challenges. The lessons I've learned and the insights I've gained are what I want to pass along to you, the reader of this book, so that you too may apply the most effective strategies of the world's greatest game to your own decision-making and use them to advance your personal and professional goals.

Why Chess?

What makes chess such an ideal laboratory for the decision-making process? To play chess on a truly high level requires a constant stream of exact, informed decisions, made in real time and under pressure from your opponent. What's more, it requires a synthesis of some very different virtues, all of which are necessary to good decisions: calculation, creativity, and a desire for results. If you ask a Grandmaster, an artist, and a computer scientist what makes a good chess player, you'll get a glimpse of these different strengths in action.

Emanuel Lasker of Germany, the second world champion, once observed, "Chess is above all a struggle." According to Lasker, the point is always to win, no matter how you define winning.

The artist Marcel Duchamp was a strong and devoted chess player. At one point he even gave up art for chess, saying the game "has all the beauty of art—and much more." Duchamp further affirmed this aspect of the game by saying, "I have come to the personal conclusion that while all artists are not chess players, all chess players are artists." And it is true that we cannot ignore the creative element, even though we have to harness it to the primary objective of winning the game.

Then we come to the scientific aspect, the one most non–chess players tend to overemphasize: memorization, precise calculation, and the application of logic. These are the bedrock of chess, and also of good decisions.

Having spent a lifetime analyzing the game of chess and comparing the capacity of computers to the capacity of the human brain, I've often wondered, where does our success come from? The answer is synthesis, the ability to combine creativity and calculation, art and science, into a whole that is much greater than the sum of its parts. Chess is a unique cognitive nexus, a place where art and science come together in the human mind and are then refined and improved by experience.

This is the way we improve at anything in our lives that involves decision-making, which is to say, everything. It's not at all surprising that the language of chess has insinuated itself into so many other pursuits. If you overheard a discussion that referred to "the opening phase," "sector vulnerability," "strategic planning," and "tactical implementation," you might assume a corporate takeover was in the offing. But it could equally refer to any weekend chess tournament. A CEO must combine analysis and research with creative thinking to lead his company effectively. A military leader has to apply his knowledge of human nature to predict and counter the strategies of the enemy.

Of course the fields of the business and military worlds are limitless compared to the confined sixty-four squares of the chessboard. But its limited scope makes chess a versatile model for decision-making. The standards of success and failure in chess are strict. If your decisions are faulty, your position deteriorates and the pendulum swings toward a loss; if they are good, it swings toward a victory. Every single move reflects a decision, and with enough time, you can analyze to a fine certainty whether each decision you made was the most effective.

Even in the complex real world, this kind of objective analysis can provide a great deal of insight into decision-making—which, ultimately, is the key to your success or failure. The stock market and the gridiron and the battlefield aren't as tidy as the chessboard, but in all of them, a single, simple rule holds true: make good decisions and you'll succeed; make bad ones and you'll fail.

I hope that the many stories I share in this book from my life in chess and, later, my career in politics will help you to gain insight into your own process as a decision-maker. I hope you will begin to formulate your own plan and continue to grow and learn. This will require great honesty in your evaluation of yourself and how well you have fulfilled your potential. There are no quick fixes, and this is not a book of tips and tricks. It is a book about self-awareness and challenge: about how you can constantly challenge yourself and others so you can learn how to make the best possible decisions.

What makes someone a better manager, a better writer, a better chess player? Not everyone performs at the same level or has the capacity to do so. What is critical is to find your own path to reach your peak; to develop your talents, improve your skills, and seek out and conquer the challenges that will push you to the highest level. And to do all this we first need a plan. In the pages that follow, you will learn how to think strategically, and how to cultivate your own, unique talents. We'll cover the more practical aspects that go into decision-making, such as understanding the crucial synergy of material, time, and quality, as well as the more human arts of memory, fantasy, and intuition. All of these elements come into play as we strive to become more creative and effective as decision-makers.

A Map of the Mind

On my sixth birthday I woke up to find an enormous globe next to my bed. It was the best present I have ever received. I had to rub my eyes to make sure it was real! I had always been fascinated by maps and geography, and my favorite childhood stories were the ones my father told me about the voyages of Marco Polo, Columbus, and Magellan. Our favorite game was to trace the journeys of these great explorers across the globe.

Before long I knew the capitals of all the world's countries, their populations, geography, industry, and everything else I could find out about them. These real adventure stories fascinated me more than any fairy tale could. I knew it must have taken incredible courage to be the first person to make the kind of journeys I read about. These stories kindled my own pioneer spirit. I wanted to blaze new trails, even if at that point in my life it meant little more than taking a new route on the walk home. Throughout my chess career I sought out new challenges, looking for things no one had done before.

The time of great explorers and emperors has passed, but there are still precious territories to discover. We can explore our own boundaries and the boundaries of our own lives. But before we go exploring, we'll need a map.

Having a personalized map of your decision-making process is essential, and this book can only roughly chart the stages of observation and analysis that go into drawing that map. The map tells you which areas of your mind are well-known to you and which are still uncharted. It reveals your strengths, weaknesses, and areas as yet untested. Most important, you must look to develop your *own* map. There is no advantage in trying to identify the common denominator that links you to your friends or colleagues or opponents. We must all look higher and dig deeper, move beyond the basic and universal. In theory, anyone can learn to play chess in half an hour, and the rules are of course the same for every man, woman, and child. When we first step beyond the rules, however, leaving that initial level where we are concerned only with making legal moves, we begin to form the patterns that distinguish us from everyone else who has ever pushed a pawn.

Acquired patterns and the logic to employ them combine with our inherent qualities to create a unique decision-maker. As time goes by, experience and knowledge are focused through the prism of talent, which can itself be sharpened, focused, and polished. This mix is the source of intuition, an absolutely unique tool that each of us possesses and that we can continuously hone into an ever-finer instrument. Here we begin to see the influence of individual psychology and our emotional makeup as it is expressed in our decisions—what we call style in a chess player.

We cannot pick and choose which style we would prefer for ourselves. Personal style is not generic software you can download and install. You must instead recognize what works best for you and then, through challenge and trial, develop your own method—your own map. To begin, ask yourself, What am I lacking? What are my strengths? What type of challenges do I tend to avoid and why? The method you employ to achieve success is a secret because it can be discovered only by you analyzing your own decisions. This is what my questioners should really have been asking me about instead of my trivial habits: How did I push myself? What questions did I ask myself? How did I investigate and understand my strengths and weaknesses? And how did I use what I learned to get better and further define and hone my method? Those are a few of the questions I have asked myself, and this book contains an honest accounting of my pursuit of the answers.

Better Decision-Making Cannot Be Taught, but It Can Be Self-Taught

Let me explain. You must become conscious of your decision-making processes, and with practice they will improve your intuitive—unconscious—performance. This is required because as adults we have already formed our patterns, good and bad. To correct the bad and enhance the good you must take an active role in becoming more self-aware.

This book will use anecdotes and analysis to open the doors to that awareness. Part I looks at the fundamental ingredients, the essential abilities and skills—strategy, calculation, preparation—that go into making effective decisions. In this section, we'll discuss how to better understand these essentials and cultivate them in ourselves. Part II is the evaluation and analysis phase. What changes are needed and why? Here we see the methods and benefits of our self-investigation. Part III examines the subtle ways we combine all of these things to improve our performance. Psychology and intuition affect every aspect of our decisions and our results. We must develop our ability to see the big picture and deal with, and learn from, the crises that we inevitably face in our lives.

Such decisive moments are turning points—every time you select a fork in the road knowing you won't be able to backtrack. We live for these moments and in turn they define our lives. We learn who we are and what truly matters to us. The "secret" then is to actively, consciously pursue these challenges instead of avoiding them. This is the only way to discover and to exploit all your gifts. Developing your personal blueprint allows you to make better decisions, to have the confidence to trust your instincts, and to know that no matter the result, you will come out stronger. There, inside each of us, is our unique secret of success.

part one

CHAPTER I

THE LESSON

Personal Lessons from the World Champion

When I first played for the chess world championship in 1984, I was a young challenger up against a champion who had held the title for almost ten years. I was twenty-one years old and had risen to the top of the chess world with such speed that I couldn't imagine that this last hurdle could block my way. I was therefore shocked when I quickly found myself down four losses without a win, only two defeats away from a humiliating rout.

If ever there was a time for a change in strategy, this was it. Instead of giving in to my feelings of desperation, I forced myself to prepare for a long war of attrition. I switched to guerrilla warfare in game after game, reducing my risks, waiting for my chance. I could not afford to expose myself in an open clash, so I played cautiously, awaiting my chance. My opponent, fellow Soviet Anatoly Karpov, fell in with my plan for his own purposes. He wanted to teach the upstart a lesson by scoring a perfect 6–0 score, so he also played cautiously instead of pressing his advantage and going in for the kill.

Karpov was also inspired by the shadow of his predecessor as champion, Bobby Fischer. En route to the title he claimed in 1972, the American had scored two perfect 6–0 wins against world-class opponents, both times without ceding even a draw. Karpov had it in mind to in some measure imitate this legendary feat when he altered his strategy against me. But conjuring Fischer's ghost turned out to be a serious mistake.

An incredible seventeen games followed without a decisive result. It appeared my new strategy was working. The match dragged on month after month, breaking every record for the duration of a world championship match. My team and I spent so much time thinking about how Karpov played, which strategies he would employ, that I uncannily felt as if I were becoming Karpov.

During the hundreds of hours of play and preparation I also got a good look at my own play, and at my own mind. Up until that point in my career everything had come easily for me, winning had simply become the natural state of things. Now I had to focus on how I made my decisions so I could fix whatever was going wrong. It was working, but when I lost game twenty-seven to go down 0–5, it looked as though I wasn't learning fast enough to save the match. One more loss and it would be three long years before I could even hope for another shot at the title.

As the match entered its third month, I stayed in my defensive crouch. I wasn't winning, but the change in style had made things much tougher for Karpov. I felt I was getting closer to solving the puzzle, while at the same time my opponent was becoming more frustrated and tired.

At last the dam broke. After surviving game thirty-one, in which Karpov failed to land a decisive blow, I won game thirty-two and went on the offensive. Another five weeks of drawn games followed, but the difference was that I was now creating more winning chances than my opponent. Meanwhile, the world began to wonder if the match would ever end. No championship match had ever gone beyond three months, and here we were entering the fifth. Karpov looked exhausted and I started to press harder. After coming close to winning game forty-six,

I won game forty-seven in crushing style. Could there be a miracle? Exactly at that moment the organizers decided the players needed a break, and the next game was postponed for several days. Despite this unprecedented decision I also won the next game. Suddenly it was 3–5 and the momentum was on my side.

Then, in a bizarre twist, on February 15, 1985, in Moscow, the president of the international chess federation (known by the acronym for its French name, Fédération Internationale des Échecs, or FIDE), Florencio Campomanes, responding to pressure from the Soviet sport authorities, called a press conference to declare that the match was canceled. After five months, forty-eight games, and thousands of hours of play and study, the match was over without a winner. We would have to return six months later to do battle again, and next time there would be a limit of twenty-four games. Karpov was removed from immediate danger and could be content that he would hold on to his title a while longer. The official press release stated that Karpov "accepted" the decision and Kasparov "abided" it. A curious but accurate semantic distinction.

I learned a huge amount from this long and grueling tutorial. In fact for five relentless months, the world champion had been my personal trainer. Not only had I learned the way he played, I was now deeply in touch with my own thought processes. I was increasingly able to identify my mistakes and analyze why I made them. From that process I learned how best to avoid making them again, to improve the decision-making process itself. This was my first real experience at questioning myself instead of relying only on my instincts.

I recognized that I had been too aggressive due to overconfidence. This in turn made me predictable. Karpov's vast experience allowed him to exploit my constant attempts to attack his position directly. He understood my play better than I understood his—and, more important, better than I understood my own. Karpov knew that I would consistently give up material for attacking chances, and he used this habit against me in that first match. Only when I began to rein in that instinct did I begin to put up effective resistance. That was the moment I first began to think about *why* I made the moves I made.

When the second match got under way in Moscow, I didn't have to wait months for my first win; I won the very first game. The match was still a tough fight—I trailed for most of the early stages—but this time I wasn't the same innocent twenty-one-year-old. I had patched the holes Karpov had so successfully exploited at the start of the first match. Now a savvy veteran at twenty-two, I became world champion and went on to hold the title for fifteen years. When I retired in 2005, I was still the highest-rated player in the world, but for a chess player forty-one is old. Still, I had remained at the summit for nearly two decades, while many of my opponents were in their teens.

Becoming Aware of the Process

It wouldn't have been possible for me to stay at the top for so long without the education Karpov gave me about my own game. Not just revealing to me the weaknesses, but the importance of finding them for myself. I didn't fully realize it at the time, but the notorious "Marathon Match" showed me the key to success. It's not enough to be talented. It's not enough to work hard and to study late into the night. You must also become intimately aware of the methods you use to reach your decisions.

Self-awareness is essential to being able to combine your knowledge, experience, and talent to reach your peak performance. Few people ever perform this sort of analysis. Every decision stems from an internal process, whether at the chessboard, in the White House, in the boardroom, or at the kitchen table. The subject matter of those decisions will be different, but the process can be very similar.

With chess having been the focus of my life from such an early age, it is no wonder that I tend to see the rest of the world in chess terms. I find that the game is usually accorded either too much or too little respect by those who look at its sixty-four-square world from the outside. It is neither a trivial pursuit nor an exercise to be left only to geniuses and supercomputers. At the heart of the game is strategy, and that is where we must begin.

CHAPTER 2

STRATEGY

The man who knows how will always have a job.
The man who also knows why will always be his boss.
—RALPH WALDO EMERSON

Success at Any Speed

Imagine learning how to play chess from a primer that's missing a few pages. The pages you have teach you how to set up the board, how to move and capture the enemy pieces, but say nothing about checkmate, nothing about the end of the game. Learning from such a book, you could become competent at calculation and proficient at maneuvering, but you'd have no higher objectives. Without a goal your play would be aimless. You might be a master tactician, but you'll have no sense of strategy.

The distinction between tactics and strategy will be important to us throughout this section. Whereas strategy is abstract and based on long-term goals, tactics are concrete and based on finding the best move right now. Tactics are conditional and opportunistic, all about threat and defense. No matter what pursuit you're engaged in—chess, business, the military, managing a sports team—it takes both good tactics and wise strategy to be successful. As Sun Tzu wrote centuries ago, "Strategy without tactics is the slowest route to victory. Tactics without strategy is the noise before defeat."

Let us begin with the big picture, with strategy. The old chess saying "A bad plan is better than no plan at all" is more clever than true. Every step, every reaction, every decision you make, must be done with a clear objective. Otherwise you can't make anything but the most obvious decisions with the confidence that the decision is really to your advantage.

In the second round of the 2001 Corus tournament in the Netherlands, I faced one of the tournament underdogs, Alexei Fedorov of Belarus. This was the strongest tournament he had ever played in, and the first time we had ever met at the board. He quickly made it clear that he did not intend to show too much respect for the august surroundings, or for his opponent.

Fedorov quickly abandoned standard opening play. If what he played against me had a name, it might be called the Kitchen Sink Attack. Ignoring the rest of the board, he launched all of his available pawns and pieces at my king right from the start. I knew that such a wild, ill-prepared attack could only succeed if I blundered. I kept an eye on my king and countered on the other side, or wing, and in the center of the board, a critical area where he had completely ignored his *development,* the term we use in chess to describe the deployment of your pieces for battle. It was soon apparent that his attack was entirely superficial, and he resigned the game after only twenty-five moves.

I admit I didn't have to do anything special to score this easy victory. My opponent had played without a sound strategy and eventually reached a dead end. What Fedorov failed to do was to ask himself early on what conditions would need to be fulfilled for his attack to succeed. He decided he wanted to cross the river and walked right into the water instead of looking for a bridge.

The lesson here is that if you play without long-term goals your decisions will become purely reactive and you'll be playing your opponent's game, not your own. As you jump from one new thing to the next, you will be pulled off course, caught up in what's right in front of you instead of what you need to achieve.

Take the 1992 American presidential campaign, the one that took Bill Clinton to the White House. During the Democratic primaries it seemed as if every day brought a new scandal that was sure to destroy Clinton's candidacy. His campaign team reacted instantly to each new disaster, but they weren't only reacting. They made sure each press release also hammered home their candidate's message.

The general election against President Bush followed a similar pattern. Against each attack the Clinton team responded with a defense that also refocused the debate on their own message—the now famous "It's the economy, stupid"—constantly reinforcing their own strategy. Four years earlier by contrast, the Democratic candidate, Michael Dukakis, had become completely distracted by his opponent's aggressive tactics. People only heard him defending himself, not presenting his own message. The 1992 Clinton team knew that it wasn't only about how quickly they responded, but how well their responses fit in with their overall strategy. Before you can follow a strategy, however, you have to develop one.

"Why?" Turns Tacticians into Strategists

The strategist starts with a goal in the distant future and works backward to the present. A Grandmaster makes the best moves because they are based on what he wants the board to look like ten or twenty moves in the future. This doesn't require the calculation of countless twenty-move variations. He evaluates where his fortunes lie in the position and establishes objectives. Then he works out the step-by-step moves to accomplish those aims.

Imagine doing that regularly at work, or even in your private activities. We all have hundreds of personal and professional objectives, but they are usually vague, unformed wish lists instead of goals that can form the basis of a strategy. "I want to make more money" is like saying "I want to find true love" or "I want to win this game." A wish isn't a goal.

To take a practical example, almost everyone at some point desires to find a better job. Only when you have a thorough understanding of why you want to change should you begin. Maybe it's not just the job, maybe you need an entirely new career. Or perhaps you can make changes at your current workplace. You won't know what you are looking for until you are aware what conditions will satisfy you.

When you do begin your search, your guide is that list of intermediate objectives that add up to your goal of "better job." For example, if money isn't your biggest issue in your current position, you shouldn't be tempted by a job that offers more cash but won't change the things that are really driving you crazy where you are now. So for every move always ask "Why?" and continue to ask it every time you come up with an answer or a new idea. It's an essential part of the chess player's discipline that can be applied to just about every pursuit in life.

These intermediate objectives are essential if we are to create conditions favorable to our strategy. Without them we're trying to build a house starting with the roof. Too often we set a goal and head straight for it without considering all the steps required to achieve it. What conditions are necessary for our strategy to succeed? What sacrifices will be required? What must change and what can we do to induce or enable those changes? And most important, why are we doing what we're doing?

In his book on Japanese business, Kenichi Ohmae summed up the role of the strategist this way: "The strategist's method is to challenge the prevailing assumptions with a single question: Why?"

"Why?" is the question that separates visionaries from functionaries, great strategists from mere tacticians. You must ask this question constantly if you are to understand and develop and follow your strategy.

When I watch novice students play chess, I'll see a terrible move and ask the student why he played it. Often he'll have no answer at all. Obviously something in his brain pushed that move forward as the best choice, but it goes without saying that it wasn't part of a deeper plan with strategic goals. Everyone would greatly benefit from stopping before each move, each decision, and asking, "Why this move? What am I trying to achieve and how does this move help me achieve it?"

Chess clearly shows us the power of "Why?" Every move has a consequence; every move either fits into your strategy or it doesn't. If you aren't questioning your moves consistently, you will lose to the player who is playing with a coherent plan.

Let us now turn our attention to tactics, the method of carrying out your strategy. Imagine a day trader who must decide "Buy or sell?" a dozen times a day. He looks at the numbers, analyzes as much as he can, and makes the best decision possible in the limited time available. The more time he spends, the better his decision will be, but while he is thinking, the opportunity to decide is passing. It's a difficult position. But his concern is mainly tactical, not strategic. Effective tactics result from alertness and speed, this is obvious, but they also require an understanding of all the possibilities at hand. Experience allows us to instantly apply the patterns we have successfully used in the past.

Tactics involve calculations that can tax the human brain, but when you boil them down, they are actually the simplest part of chess and are almost trivial compared to strategy. Think of tactics as forced, planned responses, basically a series of "if—then" statements that would make a computer programmer feel right at home. "If he captures my pawn, I will play my knight, to e5. Then if he attacks my knight, I'll sacrifice my bishop. Then if . . ." Of course, by the time you get to the fifth or sixth "if," your calculations have become incredibly complex because of the sheer number of possible moves. The chance of making a mistake increases the further ahead you look.

A tactician feels at home reacting to threats and seizing opportunities on the battlefield. When your opponent has blundered, a winning tactic can suddenly appear and serve as both means and end. Imagine a soccer game where the coaches have spent months training their players in complex strategies and set plays. But if the opposing goalkeeper slips on the grass, you toss strategy to the side and shoot for the goal without hesitation, a purely tactical reaction.

Every time you make a move, you must consider your opponent's response, your answer to that response, and so on. A tactic ignites an explosive chain reaction, a forceful sequence of moves that carries the players along on a wild ride. You analyze the position as deeply as you can, compute the dozens of variations, the hundreds of positions. If you don't immediately exploit a tactical opportunity, the game will almost certainly turn against you; one slip and you are wiped out. But if you seize the opportunities that your strategy creates, you'll play your game like a Grandmaster.

An Ever-Expanding Example

In March 2004, not long after the hundredth anniversary of the Wright brothers' famous first flight at Kitty Hawk, I gave a lecture titled "Achieving Your Potential" to an audience of executives in Interlaken, the Swiss mountain resort. To illustrate the danger of a lack of strategic vision, I chose the example of the Wright brothers and their famous invention. Hundreds of engineers had died attempting to invent a flying machine, and Orville and Wilbur succeeded, going down—or up—in history for all time.

And yet they never believed the airplane would amount to much beyond novelty and sport. The American scientific community shared that view, and soon the USA fell way behind in the aircraft business. The Wright brothers failed to envision the potential of their creation, and it was left to others to exploit the power of flight for commercial and military purposes. To this cautionary tale I added that we don't fly on Wright airplanes today. America needed someone who combined entrepreneurial vision with engineering prowess, and that man was William Boeing. More than just a strategist, Boeing was also a creative tactician.

In 1910, *American Scientific Magazine* wrote that the idea that the plane could revolutionize the world is "the wildest exaggeration." Back then, William Boeing didn't even know how to fly and was living in Seattle, Washington, far from the East Coast where most aeronautic research was going on. Boeing, who dropped out of engineering classes at Yale, didn't have the technical knowledge of the Wright brothers. What he had was a vision and the ability to develop a strategy to achieve it.

Boeing saw the commercial potential of airplanes and understood that technological excellence was the required foundation for a company that wanted to excel in—and even dominate—this new field. But to fulfill his vision several major obstacles—distance limitations and safety issues in particular—had to be overcome. Boeing bet his life savings that the technology would catch up with his vision before he went broke. But he didn't just wait around for this to happen. His strategy: better technology. His tactic: Boeing financed construction of a wind tunnel at a local university to attract the engineers he needed.

In 1917 the American military was getting ready to enter World War I. They needed planes and Boeing had a new design he thought they could use. The problem was that the navy was testing new planes three thousand miles away in Florida, too far to fly the little planes. Boeing knew that this was his crucial opportunity, so his team figured out how to take the planes apart, box them up like pizzas, and ship them across the country. It was a brilliant tactical maneuver.

That modest success allowed Boeing to continue for a few more years, during which time his struggling airplane factory also produced boats and, believe it or not, furniture. Boeing backed up his intuition about the future of commercial flight by employing countless clever tactics and maneuvers in the service of his long-term plan. He continued to hire the most talented engineers and invest in research. When mail delivery and passenger travel, plus Charles Lindbergh's sensational New York to Paris flight, created a real boom, Boeing and his superior technology were ready and waiting to dominate the industry.

Play Your Own Game

A key to developing successful strategies is to be aware of your strengths and weaknesses, to know what you do well. Two strong chess players can have very different strategies in the same position and they might be equally effective—leaving aside those positions in which a single forced winning line is available. Each player has his own style, his own way of solving problems and making decisions.

Two Soviet leading lights of opposing schools of chess thought became world champions. Mikhail Botvinnik, who first became world champion in 1948 and who would later become my teacher, trusted in immense self-discipline, hard work, and scientific rigor. His rival Mikhail Tal cultivated his wild creativity and fantasy, caring little for methodical preparation. Thomas Edison famously claimed that "genius is one percent inspiration and ninety-nine percent perspiration." This formula certainly worked for Edison and Botvinnik, but would never have worked for Tal—or for Aleksandr Pushkin, the founder of modern Russian literature. Pushkin's love of the fast life, of gambling and romance, fed his creation of some of the greatest works in the Russian language.

Tigran Petrosian, another former world champion, perfected what we chess players call prophylaxis: the art of preventative play, strengthening your position and eliminating threats. Petrosian defended so well that his opponent's attack was over before it started, perhaps even before he'd thought of it himself. His perfect defenses would leave opponents frustrated and prone to making errors, and Petrosian, alert to every small opportunity, exploited these mistakes with ruthless precision.

When I played Petrosian in the Netherlands in 1981, I was eighteen and Petrosian fifty-two. I was eager to avenge losing to him earlier in the year in Moscow, where I had developed an impressive attacking position that exploded in my face. At the time I thought it was an accident, but then it happened again. Every time it looked as if my offensive were crashing through, he would calmly make a little adjustment. All my pieces were swarming around his king and I was sure it was only a matter of time before I would land the decisive blow. But where was it? I started to feel like a bull chasing a toreador around the ring. Exhausted and frustrated, I made one mistake, then another, and lost the game. (Incidentally, something similar occurred a year later at the World Cup in Spain, when the defensive *catenaccio* style of the Italians triumphed over the attacking *jogo bonito* of the Brazilians. Sometimes the best defense is the best defense.)

I had to change my approach, and I did, inspired by an extraordinary piece of advice from the man who took the world title from Petrosian in 1969, Boris Spassky.

Spassky's own experiences against Petrosian had followed a pattern similar to mine. He first fought the defensive master for the world championship in 1966 and was turned back in a tight contest. He went into their match believing—wrongly—that Petrosian didn't play sharp, attacking chess because he lacked the skills to do so. Spassky complicated at all costs only to find his attacks brilliantly repelled by the wily world champion. Three years later, Spassky demonstrated much more respect for Petrosian's skill. In their 1969 match he played a more balanced game and triumphed.

So before I played Petrosian again, less than a year after the defeats described above, I spoke with Spassky, who was playing in the same tournament in Yugoslavia. He counseled me that the key was to apply pressure, but just a little, steadily. "Squeeze his balls," he told me in an unforgettable turn of phrase. "But just squeeze one, not both!" Over the next two years I evened the score by twice beating Petrosian with a quiet positional style, almost the style of Petrosian himself.

Those two losses had given me a deep respect both for Petrosian's abilities and for the art of defense in chess. But I also realized that such a style wasn't for me. I always wanted to be on the attacking side and my game strategies reflected that. The lesson? You must always be aware of your limitations and also of your best qualities. This knowledge allows you to both play your own game and adapt when it is required.

My aggressive, dynamic style of play fits my strengths and my personality. Even when I am forced on the defensive, I am constantly looking for a chance to turn the tables and counterattack. And when I am on the offensive, I'm not content to seek modest gains. I prefer sharp, energetic chess with pieces flying all over the board and where the player who makes the first mistake loses. Other players, including the man I defeated for the world championship, Anatoly Karpov, specialize in the accumulation of small advantages. They risk little and are content to slowly improve their position until their opponent cracks. But all of these strategies—defensive, dynamic, maneuvering—can be highly effective in the hands of someone who understands them well.

Nor is there a single best type of strategy in business. Risk-takers coexist with conservative managers at the top of Fortune 500 companies. Perhaps fifty percent of a CEO's decisions would be made in identical fashion by any competent businessperson, just as many chess moves are obvious to any strong player regardless of his style. It's that other fifty percent, or even the most complicated ten percent, where the difference is made. The best leaders appreciate the particular imbalances and key factors of each situation and can devise a strategy informed by that understanding. And they trust in what they know to be their best qualities.

Nokia CEO Jorma Ollila turned the Finnish company into the mobile phone leader with an unorthodox, even chaotic style that turned convention on its head at every opportunity. Top managers were asked to swap jobs, research and development staff met directly with customers, and the company's chief phone designer once compared its management to the way a jazz band improvises together. This flexible, dynamic approach was ideal for the fast-paced world of mobile technology.

Such a loose and energetic style might not be so successful in another industry, or another country, or with another CEO. For decades IBM built its business on a conservative, even stodgy, reputation. In the world of office machinery and mainframes that stood for reliability, which was far more important to IBM's business customers than image. New mobile phone models come out every month, while IBM was selling and servicing machines over five-year and even ten-year periods. In the eyes of their customers this very conservatism was a virtue. Rapid changes would have panicked IBM's clients.

You Cannot Always Determine the Battlefield

Of course you don't become a world champion without being able to play in different styles when necessary. Sometimes you are forced to fight on unfamiliar terrain; you can't run away when conditions aren't to your liking. The ability to adapt is critical to success.

I was forced to adapt during my advance on the road to the world championship in 1983. I was a twenty-year-old upstart taking on the fifty-two-year-old Viktor Korchnoi, a two-time world championship finalist who is still playing strong chess today at the age of seventy-five. Unsurprisingly, the veteran controlled the tempo in the early stages of our twelve-game qualification match. He won the first game and consistently prevented me from getting into the sort of open attacking positions I enjoyed.

Instead of continuing to be frustrated in my attempts to change the character of the games, I decided my best chance was to go with the flow. Instead of making sharp moves that I thought were more in my style, I played the best solid moves available even if they led to quiet positions. Freed from the psychological difficulty of trying to force the issue in each game, I could just play chess. Korchnoi forced me to fight on his terrain, but once I was conscious of it, I was able to adapt, fight, and win.

I won games six and seven to take the lead when Korchnoi decided to try to turn the tables. In game nine he switched to a tactical style, trying to surprise me with aggressive play. But having lost the battle on his territory, he wasn't able to make a successful transition to fighting on mine, and he suffered a devastating loss. This experience of adapting under fire was most helpful when I had to do the same under even less favorable conditions against Karpov in our world championship match a year later.

As any reader of Darwin knows, the failure to adapt almost always brings dire consequences. A classic example comes from American history in 1755, when George Washington was a volunteer aide-de-camp fighting in the British army against French and Indian forces. The British made almost no effort to adapt to the frontier warfare practiced by their enemies. Their general Edward Braddock was a tragically typical case. He would line up his British redcoats in orderly rows out in the open to fire well-organized volleys into the forest as the French and Indian snipers picked them off from cover. Only when Braddock himself was finally killed in a disastrous battle could his few remaining men retreat, led by none other than Washington.

Fast-forward a couple hundred years to a less calamitous story: the Encyclopaedia Britannica as it encountered the computer age. Perhaps the best-known brand name in reference books, their first blunder was to be late in releasing their products on CD-ROM. After all, they thought, who would want to replace all those beautiful books with a digitized version? Everybody, as we now know. From 1990 to 1996, sales of printed encyclopedias dropped to a tiny fraction of the reference market, and Microsoft's Encarta and others grabbed a huge market share.

Next came the Internet and its promise of almost unlimited customers around the world. Britannica charged for access at a time when everyone else was learning the market and building a customer base by giving content away for free. Britannica's business was predictably poor. A few years later the dot-com boom was busting—something I remember only too well, from my firsthand experience with my own chess Internet portal. The online advertising market collapsed entirely just as Britannica finally decided to give away their content for free. No matter what they did, they were on the wrong side of change.

What was responsible for Britannica's series of debacles? They were clearly well behind the curve when it came to moving from print to digital media. The failure of their Internet strategies is more complex. Being too far ahead of your environment can be just as bad as lagging behind your competitors. Instead of relying on their huge brand advantage they tried to outthink a new and unpredictable market and ended up fighting on a losing battlefield each time.

A Frequently Changed Strategy Is the Same as No Strategy

Change can be essential, but it should only be made with careful consideration and just cause. Losing can persuade you to change what doesn't need to be changed, and winning can convince you everything is fine even if you are on the brink of disaster. If you are quick to blame faulty strategy and change it all the time, you don't really have any strategy at all. Only when the environment shifts radically should you consider a change in fundamentals.

We all must walk a fine line between flexibility and consistency. A strategist must have faith in his strategy and the courage to follow it through and still be open-minded enough to realize when a change of course is required.

One of the tensest games of my life saw my opponent fail to have faith in his own plans. In 1985 I was locked in yet another battle with my longtime foe, Anatoly Karpov. It was the final game of our second world championship match, and I was in the lead by a single point. He had the advantage of the white pieces, and if he won, he would draw the match and retain the title for three more years.

He played aggressively right from the start and built up an impressive attacking position against my king. Then came the critical decision, whether to completely commit to his attack by pushing his pawn forward against my king side or to continue with more circumspect preparations. I think we both knew that this was the critical moment in the game.

Karpov decided against the push, and the opportunity was gone. After spending the first twenty moves of the game preparing a direct assault, he got cold feet and missed his chance. Suddenly I was in my element, counterattacking instead of defending. The game entered complications on my terms, not my opponent's, and I brought home the victory that made me the world champion.

When it came time to play for the kill, Karpov played a move that fit his prudent style but not the win-at-all-costs situation that he himself had created. His personal style was in conflict with the game strategy that was required in order to win, and he veered off course.

But Karpov is a cunning strategist and learned from his mistakes.

The lesson he took away from this critical game was to almost entirely stop opening with his king's pawn. Karpov recognized that at key moments his style wouldn't fit the sharp positions it created. He learned and adapted and stayed near the top for many, many years because he was quick to recognize that he needed to change.

Again, we return to the power of "Why?" You must know what questions to ask and ask them frequently. Have conditions changed in a way that necessitates a change in strategy or is a small adjustment all that is required? Have fundamental goals changed for some reason? Why have the conditions changed? Why are my results not as good as they once were? Avoid change for the sake of change.

Military history is full of examples of commanders who got carried away by the action on the battlefield and forgot about strategy. The French forces were routed by the English at Agincourt in 1415 when the French cavalry allowed a long-distance volley of arrows to provoke them into a disorderly charge. The French knights, out of formation and charging across muddy terrain, were repeatedly cut down. It was a downfall of arrogance. When your opponent complicates things, there is a strong temptation to look for a refutation of his idea, to pick up the gauntlet, to rise to the challenge. Of course this is exactly what he wants and why such distractions must be resisted. If you have already decided on a good strategy, why drop it for something that suits your opponent? Avoiding this trap requires extraordinarily strong self-control.

Sticking with a plan when you are winning sounds simple, but it's easy to become overconfident and get caught up in events. Long-term success is impossible if you let your heat-of-the-moment reactions trump careful planning.

An interesting side effect of my years of success was that some of my opponents chose to employ unorthodox variations to take our games into original channels. Here, they felt, my long experience would be nullified and they would be better prepared for the unusual positions. The problem, as many of these players discovered, is that most of their "original" concepts were rare for good reason. The virtue of innovation only rarely compensates for the vice of inadequacy.

Don't Watch the Competition
More Than You Watch Yourself

We must also avoid being distracted from our strategic path by the competition. If you are employing a powerful and successful strategy, whether gaining space on the chessboard or market share in global commerce, the competition will try to trip you up by getting you to abandon it. If your plans are sound and your tactical awareness is good, your competitor can only succeed with your help.

Against solid strategy, diversionary tactics will either be insufficient, or flawed. If they are insufficient, you can and should ignore them, continuing along your path. If they are radical enough to force you from your path, they are likely flawed in some way—unless you have blundered. Often an opponent is so eager to get you to change your course that he fatally weakens his own position in the attempt.

Even if the competition isn't interfering directly, we can divert ourselves. When I'm playing in a head-to-head event such as a world championship match, I only have one guy to watch and he's sitting right across the board from me. It's a zero-sum situation: I win, he loses, or vice versa. But in a tournament with a dozen players, what goes on in the other games can have an impact on my own success. It's like any business with multiple partners and competitors; if United and American airlines start talks, Continental has to pay attention.

In 2000 I was playing in a strong tournament in Sarajevo. Entering the final round, I was in the lead by the slimmest of margins, a half point. (In chess, wins are worth a point, draws half a point, losses no points.)

Two of the world's top players were right behind me, Alexei Shirov and Michael Adams. It would have been nice to face one of them for all the marbles in the final round, but we were all playing different opponents. If I drew my game and Adams or Shirov won, they would tie with me for first place. If I lost, I could drop as far as third.

So before my game I had to decide whether to play cautiously or go all out for a win. It would be heroic to enter every battle with "Victory or death" on our lips, but few situations in chess or life are as dire as when those words were written from the Alamo.

First off, I had the disadvantage of the black pieces. Next there was my opponent, an outsider in this elite event. Sergei Movsesian, representing the Czech Republic, had done poorly in the tournament but had defeated two of the highest-rated participants in the previous two rounds. I confess that our contest also had a minor personal element. The year before, writing about a tournament in Las Vegas, I had dismissed Movsesian and a few other players as "tourists," and he had taken his displeasure over my characterization to the press. Now this tourist surely wanted my scalp as a souvenir.

Then I had to consider the day's other matchups. Shirov's opponent, the Frenchman Bacrot, had already lost five games and was at the bottom of the standings. I couldn't count on him gaining a draw when his opponent had everything to play for.

Incorporating that information into my game strategy, I went on the attack from the start against Movsesian. The game was turning my way when I got up to check on my pursuers. I knew that if I won my game, how they did would be irrelevant, but it was hard not to watch. If they both drew or lost, it would be folly for me to take undue risks in my own game. In that case, I could draw and still win the tournament. Admittedly, thoughts like that made it hard to focus on my own game. There is a precarious balance between knowing what your competition is up to and becoming distracted from the factors you control directly.

Thus it was almost a relief to see that both Shirov and Adams were on the way to victory. I knew for sure that I had to ignore them and focus on my own game, and that it was now a matter of winning at all costs. As soon as I sat back down in my chair, any cautious strategies were tossed out the window. In the end, all three of us won so I kept my slim lead and took first place. Lesson: don't spend so much time worrying about the other guy that you lose sight of your own goals and your own performance.

Once You Have a Strategy, Employing It Is a Matter of Desire

Finally we come to the hardest part of developing and employing strategic thinking: the confidence to use it and the ability to stick to it consistently. Once you have your strategy down on paper, the real work begins. How do you stay on track, and how do you know when you have slipped away from thinking strategically?

We stay on track with rigorous questioning of our results, both good and bad, and our ongoing decisions. During a game I question my moves, and after the game I question how accurate my evaluations were in the heat of battle. Were my decisions good ones? Was my strategy sound? If I won, was it due to luck or skill? When this system fails, or fails to operate quickly enough, disaster can strike.

In 2000 I met a former pupil of mine, Vladimir Kramnik, in a sixteen-game match for the world chess championship, my sixth title defense. I had won the title back in 1985, and headed into this match, I had been playing some of the best chess of my life. In other words, I was ripe for defeat.

Years of success had made it difficult for me to imagine I could lose. Going into that match, I had won seven consecutive grand slam tournaments in a row and I wasn't aware of my own weaknesses. I felt I was in great form and unbeatable. After all, hadn't I beaten everyone else? With each success the ability to change is reduced. My longtime friend and coach, Grandmaster Yuri Dokhoian, aptly compared it to being dipped in bronze. Each victory added another coat.

When he played black in our match, Kramnik shrewdly chose a defense—the Berlin variation of the Ruy Lopez—in which the powerful queens quickly came off the board. The game became one of long-range maneuvering rather than dynamic, hand-to-hand combat. Kramnik had evaluated my style and had rightly assessed that I would find this kind of tranquil play boring and that I would unwittingly let down my guard. I had prepared intensely and was ready to fight on perhaps ninety percent of the chess battleground, but he forced me to play on the ten percent he knew better and that he knew I would least prefer. This brilliant strategy worked to perfection.

Instead of trying to wrest the games back to positions where I would be more comfortable, I took up his challenge and tried to beat him at his own game. This played right into Kramnik's hands. I was unable to adapt, unable to make the necessary strategic changes quickly enough, and I lost the match and my title. Sometimes the teacher must learn from the student.

In the long run I learned that I needed to be more flexible about the kinds of chess positions I enjoy. But I could have avoided this painful lesson through greater vigilance, by working harder to find and repair my weaknesses before Kramnik could exploit them.

Every leader in every field, every successful company or individual, got to the top by working harder and focusing better than someone else. The top achievers believe in themselves and their plans, and they work constantly to ensure those plans are worthy of their belief. It becomes a positive cycle, work reinforcing desire that spurs more work. Questioning yourself must become a habit, one strong enough to surmount the obstacles of overconfidence and dejection. It is a muscle that can be developed only with constant practice.

In chess we see many cases of good strategy failing due to bad tactics and vice versa. A single oversight can undo the most brilliant concepts. Even more dangerous in the long run are cases of bad strategy succeeding due to good tactics, or due to sheer good fortune. This may work once, but rarely twice. This is why it is so important to question success as vigorously as you question failure.

Pablo Picasso nailed it when he said that "computers are useless. They can only give you answers." Questions are what matter. Questions, and discovering the right ones, are the key to staying on course. Are our tactics, our day-to-day decisions, based on our long-term goals? The wave of information threatens to obscure strategy, to drown it in details and numbers, calculation and analysis, reaction and tactics. To have strong tactics we must have strong strategy on one side and accurate calculation on the other. Both require seeing into the future.

CHAPTER 3

STRATEGY AND TACTICS AT WORK

*Tactics is knowing what to do when there is something to do;
strategy is knowing what to do when there is nothing to do.*

—SAVIELLY TARTAKOWER

In the previous chapter, we discussed strategy as a clash of pieces on the board. In this one, we'll take a further step by including some psychological aspects of competition: not just how your pieces can best your opponent's pieces, but how your mind can best your opponent's mind.

In chess we have the obligation to move; there is no option to skip a turn if you can't identify a direction that suits you. One of the great challenges of the game is how to make progress when there are no obvious moves, when action is required, not reaction. The great Polish chess master and wit Tartakower half-joking called this the "nothing to do" phase of the game. In reality, it is here that we find what separates pretenders from contenders.

This obligation to move can be a burden to a player without strategic vision. Unable to form a plan when there isn't an immediate crisis, he is likely to try to precipitate a crisis himself and usually ends up damaging his own position. We learned from Petrosian that vigilant inaction is a viable strategy in chess, but the art of useful waiting takes consummate skill. What exactly do you do when there is nothing to do?

We call these phases "positional play" because our goal is to improve our position. You must avoid creating weaknesses, find small ways to

36

improve your pieces, and think small—*but never stop thinking*. One tends to get lazy in quiet positions, which is why positional masters such as Karpov and Petrosian were so deadly. They were always alert and were happy to go long stretches without any real action on the board if it meant gaining a tiny advantage, and then another. Eventually their opponents would find themselves without any good moves at all, as if they were standing on quicksand.

In life there is no such obligation to move. If you can't find a useful plan, you can watch television, stick with business as usual, and believe that no news is good news. Human beings are brilliantly creative at finding ways to pass time in unconstructive ways. At these times, a true strategist shines by finding the means to make progress, to strengthen his position and prepare for the inevitable conflict. And conflict, we cannot forget, *is* inevitable.

Europe was largely at peace entering the twentieth century, and pacifist movements were making political inroads in European parliaments. Germany meanwhile was preparing for war, and its naval buildup was matched, even provoked in some cases, by Britain's. The responsibility for this lay with one man, Admiral John "Jackie" Fisher.

Britain had quite literally ruled the waves for over a century, and in 1900 the British politicians and military leaders took this superiority entirely for granted. But Admiral Fisher insisted on modernizing the Royal Navy, building the first giant dreadnoughts and encouraging the development of submarines, which others in the Admiralty saw as sneaky and, worst of all, "un-English."

Fisher, whose bellicose personality was ill-suited to affairs of state, had to push relentlessly to achieve his program of peacetime modernization. In 1910 he retired, exhausted not by sea battles but by political battles. He was recalled by Winston Churchill at the outbreak of World War I in 1914, and although their disagreement over the Dardanelles campaign caused Fisher to resign less than a year later, his insistence on reforming the Royal Navy and making it a modern fighting force soon proved its worth.

Jackie Fisher is now recognized by historians as one of Britain's greatest admirals, and he made many of his most important contributions without firing a shot. Here was a strategist who knew that not having anything to do didn't mean doing nothing.

Element of Surprise

As Fisher's example shows, there's always an advantage in being better prepared than your opponent. But at times, your opponent will come to the game thoroughly schooled in your style and ready to counter your favorite tactics. In this case, there's another advantage you can seize: you can undo all his careful work by changing the game. In my 1995 world championship match against Indian star Viswanathan "Vishy" Anand in New York City, halfway through the match, with the score tied at one win apiece, I abandoned my favorite lines for the fearsomely named Sicilian Dragon; a defense I had never played before in a serious game.

It wasn't change for the sake of it; other factors contributed to my selection of the Dragon. It leads to an uncompromising game, one in which white must choose the most aggressive continuation to have any chance of gaining the advantage. Anand was faced with the surprise of seeing it and the knowledge that I would have prepared it extensively. In addition, our research showed that Anand had little previous experience with the Dragon and felt less comfortable against it than against other sharp opening lines. If he went for the risky main variations, he could be sure I'd have something nasty waiting for him. Instead, unable to adjust, he played tamely and lost twice.

Napoleon Bonaparte was famous for maintaining the element of surprise on the battlefield, particularly by pressing on with an attack that had apparently stalled. But he was not above using his own reputation for aggression to entrap his enemies.

Napoleon prepared for the 1805 battle of Austerlitz by retreating his forces from an excellent outpost, intentionally allowing the Russian czar's forces to move in and see the thin French lines in retreat. Young Czar Alexander decided that this was his chance for glory and prepared an all-out attack, exactly what Napoleon wanted. He had quietly brought up reinforcements to the area he had made the Russians believe to be weak.

This wasn't only a case of a clever trick working to perfection. First, Napoleon realized that he was outnumbered and that direct methods wouldn't suffice. He knew his opponent was young and impulsive and eager for glory. He also knew that no one would believe the great Napoleon would retreat from a commanding position voluntarily. Napoleon's strategy ingeniously combined all of these factors. The one-eyed Russian general Mikhail Kutuzov was the lone voice of caution, but his warnings to the czar went unheeded. Napoleon's gambit succeeded brilliantly: the czar's forces were routed in a single day.

A Genius for Development

I often refer to the need for effective development, something that is now taken for granted by any chess player beyond the rank of novice. But it took the first great American sports hero to demonstrate the importance of this fundamental concept to the world. His lesson, that you should have a solid and well-developed position before going on the attack, is applicable to every field of battle.

It seems preposterous to suggest that a single player could have a serious impact on such an ancient game in as short a time as a year. And yet in 1858 America's Paul Morphy created a legacy that altered the chess landscape forever. The wealthy young man from New Orleans entered the chess world only because he was not yet of age to practice as a lawyer when he finished his studies. He quickly proved himself in a class above the best players in the United States, but the real competition was across the Atlantic. Reversing the path of the conquistadors, the twenty-one-year-old demolished the greatest players of the day one after the other.

Morphy returned to the States as a hero. Little wonder, as he was the first American to achieve such global preeminence. While the official title of world champion wouldn't be recognized for another thirty years, there is no question that Paul Morphy was the king of chess. How did he do it? How could such a young man with no adequate competition in his native land so easily humiliate the best players in the world? Morphy's secret, and it's unlikely he was aware of it himself, was his understanding of positional play. Instead of flying directly into an attack, as was the rule in those days, Morphy first made sure everything was ready. He understood that a winning attack should only be launched from a strong position, and that a position with no weaknesses could not be overwhelmed. Unfortunately, he left no map behind, few writings that could explain his method. Morphy was so far ahead of his time that it took another quarter century for these principles of development and attack to be rediscovered and formulated.

This rediscovery was the achievement of Wilhelm Steinitz. By 1870 Steinitz had begun to develop his theories of defense, weaknesses, and strategic play. This is what divides the chess time line into "pre-Steinitz" and "post-Steinitz" periods. Although Steinitz's immortality would have been assured by his theoretical contributions, he was also successful in implementing them on the board. In 1886, he battled Johannes Zukertort, a romantic attacker of the old school, in what is now remembered as the first official world championship match. Despite losing four of the first five games, Steinitz and his principles triumphed in the end. He took the measure of his opponent, adjusted, and scored nine wins to just one further loss. Zukertort simply could not comprehend how Steinitz could win without brilliant attacks. The evolution of the game has continued, but it was Steinitz, inspired by Morphy, who first brought the game out of the sea onto dry land.

Sticking with a Plan

During my thirty years as a professional chess player we went from spending days researching an opponent by digging through musty books and journals to being able to pull up every single game in his career in seconds on a PC. It used to take months for tournament games to be published in specialist magazines. Now anyone can watch the games on the Internet in real time.

But the implications of the information revolution go much deeper than matters of convenience. With data becoming available instantaneously, our ability to deal with it must also move at warp speed. When a game is played in Moscow, it is instantly available for the entire world to analyze. An idea that took weeks to develop can be imitated by others the next day, so every player must be aware of both distant history and the immediate present and prepare accordingly. So it is harder than ever to employ surprise as a strategy on the chessboard.

In 1987 I played a six-game match of "rapid chess" on the stage of the London Hippodrome against England's Nigel Short, who would challenge me for the world championship six years later. It was the first serious match of its kind, with a greatly accelerated rate of play. In these rapid games we had just twenty-five minutes each to make all our moves, a far cry from traditional chess, where games can last up to seven hours.

I trained extensively with this new time limit and discovered that it was still possible to play deep concepts despite the impossibility of calculating deeply on each move. Instead of a profound study of a position we had to rely more on instinct. It would be fair to assume that in rapid chess careful planning and strategic goals are secondary, or even ignored, in favor of quick calculation and intuition. And I would even say that for many players this is exactly the case. If you don't like planning during a seven-hour game, you'll likely abandon it entirely in a rapid game. But the most successful players—at any speed—base their calculations firmly in strategic planning. Far from being mutually exclusive, the most effective analysis, and the fastest, is possible when there is a guiding strategy.

My battle with Short for the world championship in 1993 is a good example of sticking with a successful strategy. In my preparation we decided to take on the impetuous Englishman in maneuvering positions. He was a dangerous attacker who was well prepared in many sharp lines of play, and while this was also my strong suit, my coach and I felt I would have a considerable advantage in slower games. My analysis had revealed how uncomfortable Short was playing without activity.

In my preparation for the Short match my team and I designed my opening repertoire to steer clear of the double-edged variations he preferred. To this end I selected the slower-developing lines of the venerable Ruy Lopez opening, well-known for positional maneuvering. Named for a sixteenth-century, chess-playing Spanish priest, it has earned the nickname the Spanish Torture for its grinding effectiveness.

I started out with three wins in the first four games to take a commanding lead in the match, scheduled for twenty-four games. I had won both of my games with white using this slow maneuvering style, and many wondered if I would switch to more aggressive variations to try to knock out my opponent while he was against the ropes. Short was reeling; maybe this would be a good time to switch gears to keep him off guard.

I did make a change, but not of strategy. I used my lead to probe his defenses, looking for weaknesses. I soon scored two more wins by sticking to my strategy of opening quietly with the white pieces.

Trusting yourself means having faith in your strategy and in your instincts. When I was playing my best chess, I showed up for each contest believing the game was mine to win. I arrived at the airport with the feeling the tournament was going to have to be taken from me. In my new life in politics I continue to set ambitious goals. My chess opponents knew I was coming to the board to fight hard from start to finish, and I want my political opponents to know the same thing. The moment that confidence weakens, indecisiveness and concrete failures usually follow. If we aren't confident, we begin to postpone decisions and this leads to a destructive cycle of anxiety and time pressure.

Confidence and the Time Factor

The worst enemy of the strategist is the clock. Time trouble, as we call it in chess, reduces us all to pure reflex and reaction, tactical play. Emotion and instinct cloud our strategic vision when there is no time for proper evaluation. A game of chess can suddenly seem a lot like a game of chance. Even the finest sense of intuition can't flourish in the long term without accurate calculations.

It was March 4, 2004, and my clock was ticking down in a critical game at the most important tournament of the year, the Linares tournament in Spain. I was in second place. If I won this game, I would move into a tie for first. There were ten minutes left on my clock, and a storm was brewing on the board. I had a double-edged position against Bulgarian star Veselin Topalov, the 2005 FIDE world champion. I amassed a giant army against his king and, confident of my overwhelming power on that side of the board, launched an attack.

I saw a promising continuation but I couldn't find anything concrete in my calculations; there were too many possibilities for both sides. Eight minutes. It looked good, my intuition said it must be good. I went for it. Now it was Topalov's turn to sweat, but he proved up to the task. He defended well, setting me new problems that I had to solve in my limited time. We both played quickly, on instinct, with our hands as much as our brains. Four minutes.

Wait, was his last move a mistake? True to his combative nature, Topalov had lashed out instead of defending. To keep my attack going I sacrificed a piece, creating a serious material disadvantage. If my attack failed, I would lose the game, so there was no way back. My heart leapt and adrenaline flooded my system. I sensed the decisive blow was close at hand. With a leap of my knight I could uncover an attack by my rook against his king. It looked devastating. Where to move the knight? The e4 square or the e6 square? Forward or backward? Two minutes.

My brain was crunching through the alternatives at top speed, trying to find the best moves for both sides through the mind-bending variations. I visualized how I would counter his possible defenses, if here, then there, if this, then that. Four moves ahead, five moves, six moves . . . There was no time to analyze deeply enough to be sure of everything. One minute.

Wait, it looked as if the backward move was a losing option! Unnerved, I pushed my knight to the forward square, already sensing the opportunity was gone. Topalov reacted quickly, his king running for cover. With seconds left I could only force his king back and forth; there was no way to administer a coup de grâce. The game ended in a draw by repetition, no win, no loss. I felt deflated in my chair. Had I missed a win? After such a thrilling hunt my quarry had eluded me. I finished the tournament in a bitter tie for second place, and I was racked with concern about how my intuition had betrayed me at a critical moment.

As it turned out, I had moved my knight to the wrong square. Analysis later showed that moving it backward to e4, the "wrong" direction, away from the enemy king, would have given me an overpowering attack. I had looked at that move during my calculations but had seen that his queen could check my king, coming back to defend. When the game ended, Topalov suggested the alternative knight leap to e4 as winning, and I replied, "Yes, but what about the queen check on c1?" He looked puzzled, and just from the look on his face I suddenly realized that this move would have been illegal, the queen could not reach c_1 at all. A total hallucination. Ironically, or perhaps just cruelly, the winning move would have removed a key defensive piece, just the sort of strategic objective I would naturally have pursued had I had enough time to back it up with calculation.

The most disturbing thing about this miss was that one of the strongest parts of my game had always been fast and deep calculation—tactics. I was always confident of my ability to analyze complications better than my opponents. When it came time for me to deliver the killer blow, my adversary rarely escaped.

I left Linares with my self-confidence shaken. Of course nobody scores one hundred percent on every exam, but this was still troubling. At forty I was considerably older than most of my competitors, who were usually in their twenties and occasionally in their teens. If age was creeping up on me and my tactics were getting shaky, how much longer could I stay on top? I would have to take a close look at my game, especially my tactical abilities, before I got back on the stage.

In hindsight, I realized that the real mistake I'd made was letting myself get into such a time crunch in the first place. As later games would show, my faculties were still in fine working order. I hadn't been playing often and my rustiness had led to a lack of decisiveness, a lack of faith in my own calculations. I had spent precious minutes double-checking things that I should have played quickly. My intuition and my tactics fell out of sync. The lesson? The best plans and the most devious tactics can still fail without confidence.

Never Give In—Never, Never, Never

Winston Churchill's books are among my favorites. His tenacity—some called it stubbornness—pervaded every aspect of his character. His proposal of a military campaign in the Dardanelles during World War I—the very one that led to the resignation of Admiral Fisher—culminated in one of the worst military disasters in British history. And yet twenty-five years later he had the insight to realize that his essential idea had been correct, and he had the courage again to implement the plan.

In 1915, Churchill, then First Lord of the Admiralty, convinced the cabinet and Britain's allies to attack Gallipoli, at the heart of the Ottoman Empire, to create a supply line to Russia and to force the Germans to open a new front. Ships and troops were diverted from the Mediterranean—this is what angered Fisher—and sent to the Dardanelles, a strategic strait that divides the Asian and European parts of Turkey.

Initial naval attacks went well, but that was the end of the good news for the British. When troops were brought in, they were put under the command of Sir Ian Hamilton, who knew little of the situation on the ground. He was paired with two other commanders with no one in overall charge of the operation. One tactical blunder followed another as the British troops suffered heavy casualties against the inspired defense of the Turks, whose eventual victory led to the rise of Colonel Mustafa Kemal—later known as Atatürk—who after World War I would go on to found the Turkish Republic.

The British finally retreated after losing two hundred thousand men and three battleships. This humiliating disaster cost Churchill his job at the Admiralty, although he was called back right after the start of the next World War. In 1941, when Nazi Germany attacked the Soviet Union, Churchill realized that the Allies were facing a problem similar to that of 1915. The Soviets were low on supplies, much as Russia had been at the start of World War I. One of the first British-Soviet actions, in July 1941, was to occupy Iran to ensure overland supply lines and communication with the Soviets because they knew that the northern sea-lanes would be unsafe and insufficient in a long war.

In October, the Allies began to supply the Soviets much in the way Churchill had imagined in 1915. In 1943, this proved to be vital to the USSR's war effort, with over three hundred thousand tons of food, ammunition, and other essential supplies coming in per month. Churchill had recognized that the failure of the Gallipoli campaign didn't mean the reasoning behind it was faulty.

In his 1937 book, *Great Contemporaries*, Churchill, likely referring to a similar phrase of Samuel Johnson's, wrote that courage is the first of human qualities because it guarantees all others. To achieve success, our strategy must be implemented with accurate tactics. Our tactics should be guided by our overall strategic vision and goals. But both are only "guaranteed" by the confidence to trust the correctness of our strategy and the accuracy of our tactics. That psychological strength is the foundation. If that weakens, the entire structure falls apart.

CHAPTER 4

CALCULATION

I see only one move ahead, but it is always the correct one.

—JOSÉ RAÚL CAPABLANCA,

THIRD WORLD CHESS CHAMPION

Without a doubt, the question I am most often asked is "How many moves ahead do you see?" As with most such questions, the honest answer is "It depends," but that hasn't stopped people from asking or generations of chess players from concocting pithy replies. "As far as needed" is one, or "One move further than my opponent." There is no concrete figure, no maximum or minimum; in a way, it's like asking a painter how many brushstrokes he uses in a painting. Calculation in chess is not one plus one; it's more like figuring out a route on a map that keeps changing before your eyes.

The first reason it is impossible to reduce chess to arithmetic is because the possibilities are so numerous. For every move there might be four or five viable responses, then four responses to each of those moves, and so on. The branching of the decision tree grows geometrically. Just five moves into the game, there are millions of possible positions. The total number of positions in a game of chess is greater than the number of atoms in the universe. True, a majority of these are not realistic game positions, but the vast scope of what is possible in chess should manage to keep humans occupied for another few hundred years.

Like a weatherman's forecasts, the further ahead you look, the more likely it is you will miscalculate. We can define calculation as a sequence in which the outcome of step C depends entirely on the accuracy of our conclusions about steps A and B. Each added step into the hypothetical future increases the chance of making a mistake.

We often hear just about any type of mistake referred to as a miscalculation. It's more useful to think of this as a specific type of error, one in which the factors were known but the conclusion reached was incorrect. In chess both players know all the factors, but this is of course impossible in politics. It is still impressive how many political blunders derive from "obvious" assumptions.

Through military might and clever diplomacy, Otto von Bismarck created a German empire in the second half of the nineteenth century. After unifying Germany he managed to isolate France and cut off Russia while he allied with Austria and Italy. He was sure that France and Russia would never join forces because an absolute monarch such as the Russian czar would never "take off his hat and listen to 'The Marseillaise,'" the anthem that had accompanied the march of so many royals to the guillotine.

In 1894, four years after Kaiser Wilhelm II had replaced Bismarck as chancellor, the French signed a military alliance with Russia. And when a fleet of French ships visited Russia, the czar not only listened to "The Marseillaise" but indeed took off his hat. Bismarck had had all the information he needed, but he came to the wrong conclusion and underestimated the growing Russian economy's need for French credit. Most of all he assumed royal pride would outweigh fiscal necessity; his miscalculation had repercussions that lasted into the First World War. Bismarck was a great tactician and strategist, but in this case he failed to credit others with the same qualities. He committed the blunder of counting on his opponents to make a mistake he would never have made himself.

Calculation Must Be Focused and Disciplined

You might imagine that a game limited to a board with sixty-four squares would easily be dominated by the calculating power of today's computer technology. But as it turns out, deep calculation isn't what distinguishes the champions. Studies performed by Dutch psychologist Adriaan de Groot have shown that elite players don't in fact look ahead that much further than considerably weaker players while solving chess problems. They can, on occasion, but it doesn't define their superior play. A computer may look at millions of moves per second, but lacks a deep sense of why one move is better than another; this capacity for evaluation is where computers falter and humans excel. It doesn't matter how far ahead you see if you don't understand what you are looking at.

We have seen that precise calculation is the first key to effective decision-making. The second is the ability to evaluate both static (permanent) and fluid factors. When I contemplate my move, I don't start out by immediately running down the decision tree for every possible move. First I consider all of the elements in the position—such as material and king safety—so I can establish a strategy and develop intermediate objectives. Only when I have these goals in mind do I select the moves to analyze.

That analysis must be ordered to be effective. Anyone who has ever written down a list of errands understands that tasks can more effectively be done when prioritized and performed in optimal order. My experience guides me to select two or three candidate moves to focus on. Usually one can be discarded relatively quickly as inferior, and often another comes into consideration to take its place. Then I begin to expand the tree one move at a time, looking at the likely responses and my answering moves.

In a complicated game this tree of analysis usually stays within a depth of four or five moves—that is, four or five moves for each player, or eight to ten total moves. (We call these half moves: one move for white and one for black equals one full move.) Unless there are special circumstances—a particularly dangerous position or a key moment in a game—I know from years of experience that's a safe, practical amount of calculation.

The decision tree must constantly be pruned. Move from one variation to the next, discarding the less promising moves and following up the better ones. Don't jump to another before you've reached a conclusion on the move you're analyzing; you'll waste precious time and risk confusing yourself. You must also have a sense of when to stop. Discipline yourself to keep calculating until you have determined a path that is clearly the best, or until further analysis won't return enough value for the time spent.

Imagination, Calculation, and My Greatest Game

In some cases, the best move will be so obvious that it's not necessary to work out all the details, especially if time is of the essence. This is rare, however, and it is often when we assume something is obvious and react hastily that we make a mistake. More often you should break routine by doing more analysis, not less. These are the moments when your instincts tell you that something is lurking below the surface, or that you've reached a critical juncture and a deeper look is required.

To detect these key moments you must be sensitive to trends and patterns in your analysis. If one of the branches in your analysis starts to show surprising results, good or bad, it's worth investing the time to find out what's going on. Sometimes it's hard to explain exactly what makes those bells go off in your head telling you there is more to be found. The important thing is to listen to them when they ring. One of my best games came about thanks to this sixth sense. The scene was the strong traditional "supertournament" (roughly the equivalent of a grand slam tournament in tennis or a major in golf) in Wijk aan Zee, the Netherlands. My coactor was again the "Battling Bulgarian," Veselin Topalov.

Topalov also deserves marquee billing, because it takes two to create a truly beautiful chess game. His stern resistance pushed me to the limits of my calculation abilities in this game, in which I played the deepest combination of my career. An entire booklet dedicated to this one game was later published in Greece, and I admit that ninety percent of its analysis didn't enter my mind during the game. Once I registered a few of the exciting possibilities to chase black's king across the board, I focused and concentrated on his most likely attempts at defense. In my calculations I realized that it would be like walking a tightrope: one slip would be fatal. I would sacrifice half my pieces to flush his king out into the open. If it didn't work, I would be completely lost, so I had no choice but to invest the extra time to be as sure as possible. I kept pushing deeper into my mental image of the position, sure there must be something, until finally I saw the final winning position, an incredible fifteen moves away.

It was a feat of calculation, but there is no way your mind can go that far without help from your imagination. The combination would never have occurred to me had I taken a purely deductive approach to the position. It was not the product of logical analysis showing a mathematically perfect conclusion. As proof I can only point out that at least at one point I missed the strongest move, found in later analysis by other Grandmasters.

As an aside, although it turned out well for me, my missing the best move illustrates one of the perils of becoming fixated on a distant goal. I was so entranced by my vision of the gold at the end of this rainbow that I stopped looking around as I approached it. I'd convinced myself that such a pretty finish must be scientifically correct too—a potentially dangerous delusion.

The key to calculation is understanding its limits. You have to recognize when you are leaving the realm of what can be confirmed beyond a reasonable doubt. At that point you have to fall back on more general considerations and your intuition. In any endeavor it can be fatal to believe you are absolutely sure when in fact the situation is too complex— or the outcome too far away—to be solved by calculation alone.

CHAPTER 5

TALENT

When I was eleven, I just got good.

—BOBBY FISCHER,

ELEVENTH WORLD CHESS CHAMPION

What separates an elite chess player, one in the top ten in the world, from the many strong players who never crack the top twenty, or the top one hundred? Each player has his or her own reasons for success or failure, but the most debated among these is that most elusive quarry, talent.

There are so many definitions and aspects of talent it's little wonder we have trouble deciding who has it and who doesn't. Prodigies make this easy, but we can do little more than marvel at the likes of Mozart, who composed symphonies at age five, and Pascal, who was creating original geometric theorems on the walls of his childhood home at twelve.

Chess, along with music and mathematics, is one of the few pursuits in which superior ability and originality can manifest at a young age. José Capablanca reputedly learned the game at the age of four just by watching his father play and soon proved a match for accomplished players. Polish-born Samuel "Sammy" Reshevsky was trotted out in a sailor suit to give exhibitions at the age of seven, defeating entire roomfuls of adult players all across Europe. Reshevsky was poked and prodded by every type of psychologist in a search of the source of his miraculous abilities. How could mere children master a game that was synonymous with complexity and difficulty?

We are all familiar with tales of such precocity and are in general willing to accept that these individuals are born with special gifts. Still, even their extraordinary talents require the opportunity to develop. Had his father been a painter instead of a music teacher, would we know of Mozart today?

My own development certainly owed a great deal to external factors. I grew up in Baku, Azerbaijan, then part of the loose Soviet empire. It was a typical imperial outpost, a rich melting pot of ethnicities that was somewhat flattened by a common language and a dominant Russian/ Soviet culture. My own roots were characteristic—an Armenian mother, Klara Kasparova, and a Jewish father, Kim Weinstein—what they call an explosive combination. The atmosphere in our household was a combination of my mother's rigid pragmatism mixed with my father's contrarian creativity. The rest of the clan included my father's brother, Leonid, and their cousin Marat, a famous lawyer in Baku. Their circle largely consisted of professors and intellectuals who constantly questioned the official view, not only the blatant propaganda of the Soviet government. For them, the conventional wisdom was to be doubted out of hand— everything should be subjected to questioning.

We would listen to Radio Liberty and Voice of America, and I remember getting into great debates with Grandpa Shagen, my mother's father, who did not take kindly to views critical of the state. He had spent his whole life building Communism, and so the food shortages of the late 1970s were to be a source of great disillusionment for him. Between these poles I grew up reading a lot of books and asking a lot of questions. When my father died, I went to live with my mother's family. When I began to have public success in chess, it seemed natural to take her family name. My teacher Botvinnik, himself of Jewish ancestry, added that it wouldn't hurt my chances of success in the USSR not to be named Weinstein.

My father was the first to recognize my natural aptitude for chess.

He was struggling with leukemia when he made his last decision, which was to send me for chess schooling at the age of seven. My mother enthusiastically supported my development. Nowadays she likes to remind me how her efforts were more often directed at controlling my willfulness than promoting it. She tells the story of a phone call she received from my second-grade teacher, who had chastised me for challenging her in class. The teacher told me I should not do this because it would make everyone think I believed I was the cleverest in the class. To which I replied, "But isn't that true?" I do not envy my former teachers.

Just about every young star in any field can give credit to a determined parent giving talent a push. As for internal factors, it is clear to me that I would not have achieved such success at anything other than chess. The game came to me naturally, its requirements fitting my talents like a glove. My talents for memorization and calculation were blended with an aggressive streak for an ideal chess combination.

Recognizing the Patterns in Our Lives

What we refer to as "talent" is actually a set of attributes, not just a single on-off switch. A concert pianist needs physical dexterity as well as a good ear and a sense of rhythm. Most things can be broken down into such skill sets. Think about what it takes to be a good manager, a good general, a good parent. Chess is no exception, and to excel at it requires a synthesis of developed talent and acquired knowledge. It may seem an unusual pairing, but as the most important innate qualities I would cite memory and fantasy. These are the qualities the greatest players exhibited in abundance.

People often talk about a good memory as if it were something you either possess or you don't, such as height or blue eyes. Many try to categorize it, saying they have a good memory for faces or a bad memory for names. We perpetuate stereotypes like the absentminded professor who has memorized the complete works of Chaucer but can't remember where he parked his car.

We know that the brain stores long-term and short-term memories in different places. There are stories of people with total recall who are capable of effortlessly reciting entire phone books. People often believe that elite chess players must possess such faculties, but this is far from the truth.

It's true that to be a great chess player you must have a good memory, but it is much harder to explain what, exactly, we are remembering. Patterns? Numbers? Mental pictures of the board and pieces? The answer seems to be "all of the above."

The practice of "blindfold chess" has fascinated the world for centuries. In 1783, the great French player François-André Danican Philidor played two games simultaneously without sight of the boards and was acclaimed a genius without parallel. One newspaper account described it as "a phenomenon in the history of man and so should be hoarded among the best samples of human memory, till memory shall be no more." Certainly it is impressive to see a man with his back to the boards—or more theatrically, literally blindfolded—calling out strong moves and overwhelming his opponents who are seated at the board. But it is no miracle.

Nearly two hundred years later, the Polish Grandmaster Miguel Najdorf was stranded in Argentina at the outbreak of World War II. When the war ended, Najdorf had the idea of trying to communicate word of his survival to his family in Poland by staging the largest exhibition of blindfold chess ever attempted, on forty-five boards simultaneously. That's 1,440 pieces to keep track of. After nearly twenty-four hours of play, Najdorf scored thirty-nine wins, four draws, and just two losses against his opponents, all of whom had full sight of the board.

This is not to say that Najdorf had a perfect, photographic memory;

he did not. What he had was a remarkable "chess memory," the ability to retain the patterns and movements of pieces on a sixty-four-square board, which is as essential to a player when he can see the board as when he cannot. This capacity for recall and visualization makes our calculations quick and accurate and means we don't have to rely on calculating every position from scratch. If you are familiar with a similar position and can remember what worked or didn't work before, you have a big advantage over someone who is seeing it for the first time. The position doesn't have to be an exact replica to produce this benefit. If you play the Najdorf Defense your entire career, you develop a feel for what moves to make and when in response to certain ideas and plans. We automatically find parallels and apply our knowledge of analogous positions.

A Grandmaster will retain tens of thousands of fragments and patterns of chess data and adds to them constantly through frequent practice. My ability to recall so many games and positions doesn't mean I have an easier time remembering names, dates, or anything else. De Groot illustrated this in an elegant fashion in his 1944 study of chess players. He tested players of every level, from former world champions to beginners, seeking to unlock the secrets of master chess.

He gave the players a set of positions from games to memorize, then recorded how well they could reproduce them. Predictably, the stronger the player, the better he scored. The elite players scored ninety-three percent, the experts seventy-two percent, the average players just 51 percent.

Thirty years later, in 1973, researchers Bill Chase and Herb Simon replicated de Groot's experiment but added a key second set of test positions. For the second set they placed the pieces on the boards randomly, not following the rules of the game or any pattern at all. As in de Groot's study, the stronger players scored better on the positions taken from actual games. But with the random positions, all levels of players scored approximately the same. Without being able to utilize patterns, or what psychologists call chunks, the masters didn't display superior memory prowess.

The same processes are at work in every human endeavor. Rote memorization is far less important than the ability to recognize meaningful patterns. When we tackle a problem, we never start from scratch; we instinctively, even unconsciously, look for a past parallel. We work out the authenticity of the parallels and see if we can work out a similar recipe from these slightly different ingredients.

Traders see trends in the graphs of a stock, parents observe patterns of behavior in their children, an experienced courtroom lawyer can intuit the most effective way to handle a witness. All derive from a combination of experience and consciously observed memory. And while practice alone can make you competent, to excel requires actively examining what you are retaining.

How often do you review your performance at the end of the day? What did you see, what did you learn? Did you observe or experience something new that's worth taking note of? Would you recognize that situation, that opportunity, that pattern, should it occur again? Elite performers such as Olympic athletes must be this critical, this self-aware, to succeed.

The benefits of such rigorous behavior aren't so obvious if you work in an office, but they are there just the same. Even people in leadership roles are too often content to just get through the day. Most people talk about unwinding after work or school, putting the day behind them so they can relax. How much more effective would they become if, at the end of each day, they asked themselves what lessons they had taken away for tomorrow?

We can do a great deal to make our own luck when it comes to matching our abilities with our careers. The problem is that as we get older and more settled in our ways and our professions, we rarely test our resources. And without constant testing it is impossible to discover what our gifts are. I believe it's essential to push the boundaries and constantly widen the angle of the lens we use to view the world. One crucial way to do that is through what I call creative experimentation.

The Power of Fantasy

Tal doesn't move the pieces by hand; he uses a magic wand.
—GRANDMASTER VIACHESLAV RAGOZIN,
TRAINER OF WORLD CHAMPION MIKHAIL BOTVINNIK

The French novelist Anatole France wrote that "to accomplish great things, we must dream as well as act." In chess we have a name for the sort of imagination required to break out of the usual patterns and startle our opponents; we call it fantasy. This is where we let our mind drift away from the calculation of variations to imagine hidden possibilities in the position. Occasionally we can find a novel idea that all but breaks the rules—one that finds a way to use the unique confluence of factors on the board at that exact instant to brilliant advantage.

Ironically, chess computers are good at producing moves that strike humans as full of tactical fantasy. Computers don't rely on patterns and hold no prejudices against moves that are ugly or appear illogical or absurd. They simply count the beans and play the best move they find. It's much harder for a human being, a creature of habit, to be so brutally objective.

Fantasy Can Cut Through Fog

Keeping an open mind is difficult in a game where so much depends on patterns and logic. For inspiration I look to those great players who consistently found original ways to shock their opponents. None did this better than the eighth world champion, Mikhail Tal. The "Magician of Riga" rose to become champion in 1960 at age twenty-three and became famous for his aggressive, volatile play. He would sacrifice pawns and pieces in ways that went completely against the grain of the modern, scientific era of the game established by Botvinnik. Tal reinvented the romantic form of chess, the way it was played back in the mid-nineteenth century, when defense was considered cowardly.

How did he do it? How could it be that Tal's knights seemed more agile, and his bishops faster, than those of other Grandmasters? He was a tremendous calculator, but that was only a small part of his gift. He had the ability to realize when calculation alone wasn't going to solve the problem. Here's how he described a classic game against the Soviet Grandmaster Vasiukov, in which he was contemplating a knight sacrifice.

Ideas piled up one after another. I would transport a subtle reply to my opponent, which worked in one case, to another situation where it would naturally prove quite useless. As a result, my head became filled with a completely chaotic pile of all sorts of moves, and the famous "tree of variations," from which the trainers recommend that you cut off the small branches, in this case spread with unbelievable rapidity.

And then suddenly, for some reason, I remembered the classic couplet by [well-known Soviet children's poet] Korney Chukovsky:

Oh, what a difficult job it was
To drag out of the marsh the hippopotamus.

I don't know from what associations the hippopotamus got onto the chessboard, but although the spectators were convinced that I was continuing to study the position, I was trying at this time to work out: Just how would you drag a hippopotamus out of the marsh?

I remember how jacks figured in my thoughts, as well as levers, helicopters, even a rope ladder. After a lengthy consideration, I admitted defeat as an engineer, and thought spitefully, "Well, let it drown!" And suddenly the hippopotamus disappeared. Went off from the chessboard just as he had come on. Of his own accord. And straightaway the position did not appear to be so complicated. Now I somehow realized that it was not possible to calculate all the variations, and that the knight sacrifice was, by its very nature, purely intuitive. And since it promised an interesting game, I could not refrain from making it.

And the following day, it was with pleasure that I read in the paper how Mikhail Tal, after carefully thinking over the position for forty minutes, made an accurately calculated piece sacrifice.

It's a charming example of Tal's wit, and more important, an insight into his problem-solving method. He realized that he was wrong to attempt to fix with a wrench something that required a hammer. Even his imaginative mind occasionally required a push to shift into a different gear. And most important, he allowed himself to follow this line of fantastical thinking in the heat of battle.

Developing the Habit of Imagination

Fantasy isn't something you can turn on with the flip of a switch. The key is to indulge it as often as you can to encourage the habit, to allow your unconventional side to flourish. Everyone develops his own device for prompting his muse. The goal is for it to become continuous and unconscious, so your fantasy is always active. It's not about being an inventor, with an occasional flash of creativity, but about being innovative in your decision-making all the time.

While the name Joseph Wilson might not ring a bell, the company he led, Xerox, certainly will. Wilson was himself an inventor, but the creative attitude he brought to the company, originally named Haloid Co., was more important than anything Wilson created in a laboratory. He used to tell new employees, "We do not want to do things in the same old way. Therefore, as you come here, I hope that you come with an attitude that change will be a way of life for you. You will not do things tomorrow the way you are doing them today." He later established the famed Palo Alto Research Center (PARC), which pioneered the earliest versions of the personal computer, the mouse, and the graphical user interface.

From my old chess training routines to my sleeping patterns, I confess to being a creature of habit, so it requires considerable effort for me to take Wilson's advice. At the board I always tried to let my mind wander, to occasionally ignore the fog of variations and take a mental stab in the dark. In a competitive situation such moves—today we might call them thinking outside the box—have the added benefit of often coming as a complete surprise to your opponent. The time he has spent thinking on your move has mostly been wasted, and the landscape of the game has changed. It's more than playing a good move, an objectively strong move. Moves with an extra charge of fantasy can startle your competition into making mistakes. Here's an example.

In 1997 I was playing in a tournament in Tilburg, the Netherlands, and in the fifth round I had the black pieces against one of the world's leading "fantasy players," the Latvian-born Alexei Shirov, who now plays for Spain. The creative Shirov was trained in his early years by Mikhail Tal himself, a pedigree without peer when it comes to exotic attacking play.

This time, however, I gave him a taste of his own medicine. In a complicated position with chances for both sides, Shirov moved his rook up the board, preparing to attack my queen on the next move. I obviously had to get my queen out of the way, and I sat looking at the few possible retreats. All the options would leave the position dynamically balanced, but I was disappointed there wasn't the opportunity for more.

Before I resigned myself to the seemingly inevitable queen move, I took a deep breath and surveyed the rest of the board. As with so many fantasy moves, this one started with a mental "Wouldn't it be nice if . . ." If you daydream a little about what you'd like to see happen, sometimes you find that it is really possible. What if I ignored his threat to my queen? He would have extra material, but my pieces, while technically outgunned by his queen, would be active and he'd be under pressure.

So instead of picking up my queen, my hand lifted my king and moved it a single square toward the center of the board. The paradox was satisfying, ignoring all the action and threats to play an innocuous-looking move with the weakest piece on the board. Of course I was also sure that it was a strong move on its own merits. Fantasy must be backed up by sober evaluation and calculation or you spend your life making beautiful blunders.

Shirov didn't adapt well to the new situation. A born attacker, he was suddenly on the defensive. The position was objectively about even, but he quickly made a serious mistake, and it didn't take long to wrap up the game after that. I had the pleasure of sacrificing even more material at the very end to finish things off with a flourish.

Too often we quickly discard apparently outlandish ideas and solutions, especially in areas where the known methods have been in place for a long time. The failure to think creatively is as much self-imposed as it is imposed by the parameters of our jobs and of our lives. "What if?" often leads to "Why not?" and at that point we must summon our courage and find out.

Be Aware of Your Routines, Then Break Them

There are as many ways to engage your fantasy as there are decisions to be made during a day. You won't find new ways of solving problems unless you look for new ways and have the nerve to try them when you do find them. They won't all work as expected, of course. The more you experiment, the more successful your experiments will be. Break your routines, even to the point of changing ones you are happy with to see if you can find new and better methods.

In the competitive chess world I had clear standards for success and failure. That meant it was relatively easy to determine what worked and what did not. Trial and error led me to establish and refine my successful routines. When I had a poor result, I knew it was time to reexamine these things, both in my chess and in my day-to-day life. Without obvious benchmarks for success and failure it is even more important to have a constant process of reevaluation.

CHAPTER 6

PREPARATION

If a man has a talent and cannot use it, he has failed.
—THOMAS WOLFE

Like the proverbial tree falling in the forest with no one around to hear, talent undiscovered may as well not exist. That being the case, we can hardly lament its loss. We can, however, mourn the talent that goes undeveloped, talent that exists but is squandered. In contrast, we often reserve the highest praise for those who overachieved with limited natural abilities, those who outworked and outperformed rivals who possessed greater innate gifts.

That last tendency has always struck me as unfair. Why isn't the capacity for hard work considered a natural gift? I don't think it's a compliment to say that someone "did more with less," even though it's usually intended that way. If a soccer player who is short and can't run fast practices more than everyone else and becomes the superior player, has he overcome a talent deficit or simply exploited his talent to work harder and found a way to be successful through determination and focus?

Michael Jordan was famous for his athleticism and high-flying dunks, yet he was also the first to arrive at practice and the last to leave. In interviews, Jordan's teammates and coaches all talk about his extreme discipline, not his leaping ability. One veteran NBA manager said of Jordan's talent, "Without the ceaseless work ethic, Jordan is merely another talented athlete gliding through an admirable career, but nothing historic."

I agree, but again this makes it sound as if Jordan's discipline and capacity for work are not intrinsic parts of his talent. The ability to push yourself to the limit day after day, and to do so effectively, may not be as evident as physical skills, but it was something Michael Jordan cultivated his entire career and is a talent that we should all try to cultivate.

Results Are What Matter

Throughout my chess-playing life, people complimented me—sometimes in a backhanded way—on the depth and breadth of my preparation. In this way, I was part of a proud lineage. In the 1920s, Alekhine worked harder than anyone before him, changing the culture of a gentleman's game. For his efforts he was often branded "obsessed" by those he defeated. In the 1940s, Botvinnik's rigorous mind and habits transformed the game into a full-time profession. In the 1970s, Fischer's fantastic dedication forced every other player to spend more time studying or be left behind.

My work ethic developed from the disciplined environment created by my mother and my teacher Botvinnik. I had a ceaseless appetite for opening preparation, which combines research, creativity, and memorization. I studied all the latest games from the leading players and carefully noted their innovations. Then, I would analyze them and try to improve on them. To me the opening systems were an avenue for creativity, not simply a matter of imitation.

My training sessions with coaches as a youngster helped form my sense of discipline. Goals were set and certain hours on my schedule were allocated for work on the openings, for example. It was clear to me at a young age that such work paid concrete dividends and that without it I would be squandering my abilities. Botvinnik had no patience for brilliant ideas that weren't backed up with exhaustive analysis. I learned to enjoy the study and analysis process itself and not just to see it as a necessary evil or means to an end. Over time I came to relish my preparation time because it gave me the feeling that while my competitors were sleeping, I was improving.

Not long after my explosive entry into the international chess world, I started to hear whispers that credited much of my success to deep study with a Soviet team. In the years that followed, this developed into a full-scale myth. "Kasparov has a team of Grandmasters churning out opening novelties day and night!" "He has a supercomputer!" After a while it started to grate to hear these things repeated to me in interviews, although I tried to take them as compliments. As with most urban legends, however, these stories have a grain of truth.

It has long been common for top players to work with analytical assistants—called seconds, as in the days of duels—especially during world championship matches. When I had the resources to do so, I began to work with a trainer full-time and not only right before and during big events. As for my computer, I was the first player to incorporate machine analysis into my preparation and to systematize the use of playing programs and databases. And while it was the best my techie cousin Eugeni could put together, the PC I used was never beyond the reach of anyone with a good computer store nearby.

Instead of listening to what people said about how I achieved them, I focused on the results. The concrete methods I used—a fixed number of hours per week for specific training tasks, for example—wouldn't work for everyone, but they worked well for me. If critics and competitors can't match your results, they will often denigrate the way you achieve them. Fast, intuitive types are called lazy. Dedicated burners of midnight oil are called obsessed. And while it's obviously not a bad idea to hear and consider the opinions of others, you should be suspicious when these criticisms emerge right on the heels of a success.

Inspiration vs. Perspiration

Everyone, at any age, has talents that aren't fully developed—even those who reach the top of their profession. The Cuban Capablanca was, for example, considered an invincible chess machine. There's some truth to this: he once went eight years without a defeat. But Capablanca, if not perhaps as lazy as the legend (and his own claims) would have it, detested study. A bon vivant whose expenses were covered by a sinecure with the Cuban diplomatic office, he rarely prepared for his opponents and liked to brag that he had never seriously studied. He was confident he could escape from any trap he fell into, and he was usually right.

When Capablanca took the crown from Lasker in 1921, it was considered an overdue coronation for a reign that could last decades. "Capa" made chess look easy, and for him it was. But he relied too much on his native ability, and his grip on the title lasted only six years. Fittingly, his conqueror, the Russian Alexander Alekhine, was one of the most fanatically dedicated players the game has ever seen.

In an age when the gentleman chess player was still common and chess as a profession was considered questionable, Alekhine made chess his life as no one had before. There's an old story about a patron who invites Capablanca and Alekhine to the theater and comments afterward, "Capablanca never took his eyes off the chorus; Alekhine never looked up from his pocket chess set!"

Of course Alekhine had his own fiery genius at the board, and by combining that with his intense dedication he was more than a match for the raw talent of Capablanca. He had made a careful study of all of Capablanca's games, and though he found few specific weaknesses to exploit, he did find occasional errors that gave the lie to the myth of Capablanca's invincibility.

Even so, Alekhine considered Capablanca the favorite going into their 1927 match in Buenos Aires. He had never before defeated the mighty Cuban and had finished a distant second behind Capablanca at the New York tournament earlier that year. And yet that easy victory was part of Capablanca's undoing.

Capablanca lost the first game in Buenos Aires, and although he came back to briefly take the lead, he must have been surprised to find himself in such a bitter fight. The match became a test of wills, and here Alekhine, who once said, "What I do is not play, but struggle," was in his element. The drive that led him to prepare eight hours a day "on principle" would not let him lose. Capablanca was unused to such strenuous effort and finally went down to defeat after thirty-four games. (A record that would stand until my 1984–85 match with Karpov lasted forty-eight games.)

As Alekhine later wrote of their match, "I did not believe I was superior to him. Perhaps the chief reason for his defeat was the overestimation of his own powers arising out of his overwhelming victory in New York, 1927, and his underestimation of mine."

As a cautionary epilogue, we should also keep in mind that Alekhine himself could let down his guard. Alekhine's overindulgence of alcohol damaged his health and his career—many credit his shocking (and brief) loss of the title to Max Euwe in 1935 to this as much as to his Dutch challenger's strong play and deep preparation. No longer underestimating his opponent, and on a strict regimen of milk, Alekhine reclaimed the title two years later.

Preparation Pays Off in Many Ways

We can't all have the single-minded dedication of an Alekhine. Few lives and few endeavors permit such devotion. But in truth it's not the amount of time that really counts—it's the quality of your study and how you use your time. Becoming a 24/7 fanatic who counts every minute and second isn't going to make you a success. The keys to great preparation are self-awareness and consistency. Steady effort pays off, even if not always in an immediate, tangible way.

One interesting, and humbling, thing I've noticed while analyzing my own games for publication is how poor some of the ideas I prepared really were. From the safety of retirement I now look back at the huge amount of analysis I did in preparation for my tournaments and world championship matches. Only a fraction of these ideas ever saw the light of day, either because my opponent didn't fall into my trap or because in the heat of battle I found a better variation to play. Now I see that in many cases that was not a bad thing. With the benefit of powerful computer programs, it becomes clear that instead of wielding Excalibur, I was in many cases preparing to charge the enemy with a rusty pocketknife. Still, this kind of preparation served me well in a way I never quite appreciated while I was working on it with such determination. These periods of intense preparation were rewarded with good results—even when I didn't end up utilizing the fruits of my labor. There was an almost mystical correlation between work and achievement, with no direct tie between them. Perhaps I was benefiting from the chess equivalent of the placebo effect. Going into battle with what I believed were lethal weapons gave me confidence even though they went largely unused and wouldn't in some cases have been effective.

There is also a practical benefit to such "wasted" effort. The research a lawyer does preparing for a case that never goes to trial still enriches his understanding of the law and makes him better at his job. Work leads to knowledge, and knowledge is never wasted. Even if our weapons remain sheathed, our opponents know they exist and may be distracted by the potential for nasty surprises.

This ethic has been followed by many people known to history as great geniuses. We cannot doubt the brainpower of Thomas Edison, but his true genius lay in his capacity for endless experimentation. In creating the electric lightbulb, he tested thousands of substances to find a filament that wouldn't burn out, even working with rare plant fibers sent in from around the world. "Opportunity," Edison said, "is missed by most because it is dressed in overalls and looks like work." This was an echo of another great thinker and worker, Thomas Jefferson, who wrote, "I'm a great believer in luck and I find the harder I work, the more I have of it."

The worst of it is that we are usually aware of our deficiencies when it comes to practice and hard work. We criticize ourselves harshly after spending an hour at work surfing the Web or for leaving the gym bag by the door while we watch television. But of course this self-flagellation produces no more benefit than those New Year's resolutions that rarely outlast the winter. Before you tell yourself you don't have the talent of a Jordan or an Alekhine, remember the extraordinary amount of time they devoted to practice and study. To succeed like them you must put in the effort they did. Otherwise, you can never know what you're capable of. I believe that if opportunity isn't provided at a young age, it can be created later in adulthood through discipline and imaginative involvement in the pursuits we care about. You can—and must—look for ways to experiment and to push the boundaries of your capacity in different areas.

Turning a Game into a Science

If Alekhine brought a new level of dedication, even obsession, to the game of chess, the man who succeeded him on the throne professionalized and codified this devotion. The first of the seven Soviet champions, Mikhail Botvinnik sought to demystify the game through his writing and teaching.

Botvinnik's most lasting contributions to chess culture were in the area of preparation. Ever the engineer, he established detailed training regimens. These encompassed not only specific chess research, but also physical and psychological preparation. These methods are so commonplace now it is hard to imagine a time when every player didn't do these things, but at the time Botvinnik was a true innovator. His system involved researching the opening phase of the game, studying his opponents' styles, and rigorous analysis of his own games, which were published so they could be criticized by others. To give just one example of the extremes he would go to: during training sessions for a tournament Botvinnik would have distracting music playing in the background and even requested that one of his trainers, Ragozin, blow smoke in his face.

I was Botvinnik's favorite pupil at the chess academy, and I owe a great deal to him for adding focus and discipline to my natural aptitude. He taught me to avoid complexity for complexity's sake, saying, "You will never become an Alekhine if the variations control you and not the other way around." So Botvinnik laid out the ideal tournament regimen, establishing a strict timetable for meals, rest, and brisk walks, a system I followed my entire career. If you said you didn't have enough time, that meant you were not well organized. And forget about telling the great teacher you were tired that day! Sleep and rest were to be as carefully scheduled as training, and it was simply inexcusable to get insufficient rest. Botvinnik summed up his philosophy by stating, "The difference between man and animal is that man is capable of establishing priorities!"

I was lucky because I had been well prepared for Botvinnik by my mother, Klara, who inherited a strong sense of the importance of order and routine from her family. For me it was simply the way things were, and I always felt comfortable with it. Sleep, meals, school, study time, recreation time, all were part of a schedule.

Of course it was easier thirty years ago when I was growing up. There were fewer distractions available, fewer acceptable activities for a child, especially in the USSR. Today distractions are virtually unlimited, and the computerized world makes instant entertainment ubiquitous and available to everyone. Mobile phones, video games, and gadgets allow us to waste time in a dozen different ways that don't usually add up to anything at all.

With so much activity in their own lives, parents have few opportunities to teach, let alone demonstrate, rules and regimen and to present a good example. I could observe the way my mother programmed her life and my activities, and I had no doubt it was all for the best.

As I grew older and moved into the serious chess world as a young teenager, I continued to be surrounded by hardworking coaches and mentors. Botvinnik's words and example strengthened what I had already learned from my mother. He provided the game plan, helping me to develop the routines and practices that reinforced a general ethic about hard work and dogged preparation.

Now, though retired from professional chess, I stick with my routine as closely as possible. This means hours of sleep, mealtimes, hours of work on different projects, and staying conscious of how these things are balanced daily and weekly. I've adapted my new activities into the old chess program, preserving the patterns that have kept me comfortable and productive. Where there used to be chess, there is now politics. Where before I would analyze the games of my chess opponents, I now analyze the statements of my political opponents. My afternoon nap is still sacrosanct.

Targeting Ourselves for Efficiency

Alekhine and Botvinnik, and later Bobby Fischer, had a talent for working constantly and effectively. They could keep pouring more energy in and getting positive results back out. We can all work longer hours, study more, watch less TV, but the ability to remain effective under increasing strain varies from person to person. Everyone has a unique level of efficiency in his ratio of work to results. A Capablanca might be creative for an hour but burn out after two. An Alekhine might need four hours to get those same results, but is capable of working for eight hours without a drop in productivity.

It is critical to know what motivates you, to find out how to push yourself that extra mile. For me it's sticking to a regimen. As long as I don't make exceptions to my program, I feel motivated. I also know that I need new challenges to stay engaged. The minute I begin to feel something has become repetitive or easy, I know it's time to quickly find a new target for my energy.

Others use different devices, such as competition, setting goals, or using incentives. Anatoly Karpov was not by nature a hard worker, but he spent ten to twelve hours a day preparing for his match with Boris Spassky in 1974. Karpov is tremendously competitive, and his will to win spurred him to new levels of effort. It paid off and he beat Spassky convincingly.

If discipline sounds dull, or even impossible in today's fast-paced world, you should take a moment to consider how you might benefit from targeting just a few small areas of your life for efficiency. Having a good work ethic doesn't mean being a fanatic, it means being aware and then taking action. If you spend fifteen minutes a day studying openings, in a year you'll be a stronger chess player. If you spend an hour a day learning Mandarin, in a few years you may be ready for an entirely different career.

This isn't a cookbook, and I'm not offering a recipe for your success. Everyone must create his own successful combinations with the ingredients he has. There are guidelines for what works, but each person has to discover what works for him. This doesn't happen by itself. Through practice and observation, you must take an active role in your own education.

With the fundamental ingredients behind us we move now to the evaluation and analysis phase of decision-making. Knowing what to look for is only the first challenge. Good decisions require the ability to weigh all of the factors present and to decide the best balance among them.

part two

CHAPTER 7

MTQ: MATERIAL, TIME, QUALITY

Every chess player is familiar with the concepts of material, time, and quality. The balance among these three factors is the foundation of every move in chess—and in every decision we make. Making a correct evaluation—and then a correct decision—requires understanding the trade-offs and relative values of these core elements. Material describes our tangible assets. Time is how long it takes to achieve a specific objective. Quality, the most important element and a goal unto itself, is value—or even power. We strive to gain in every area and also to invest and balance the factors correctly.

Evaluation Trumps Calculation

It was a curious experience when I first tried to think seriously about what exactly goes through my mind when I look at a chess position. After a lifetime of living and breathing the game, I can only compare it to trying to understand what happens in your brain as you read this book. For me, chess is a language, and if it's not my native tongue, it is one I learned via the immersion method at a young age. Like a native English speaker trying to explain the difference between *that* and *which*, such familiarity makes it difficult for me to consider my approach to the game objectively. Now that I'm removed from the heat of battle and tournament play, I can look back at my games and performances with greater introspection and better understand what goes into strategic assessment.

Improving your decision-making is like studying your native language. Even though most of us don't know much about the mechanics of the language we learned as children, that doesn't prevent us from speaking it fluently. But still, we all make mistakes: incorrect grammar, words we use improperly, awkward sentences. Millions of books on more effective writing are sold every year to native speakers who recognize the value of communicating with greater precision. Similarly, with decision-making we all have an apparatus that gets us through life. But there are still improvements that can (or is it may?) be made.

To do so requires conscious thought about something you've done unconsciously all your life. Since the day you started to crawl, you've been making countless choices, and like the rest of us, you've developed systems and tendencies that you employ instantly, constantly, without being the least bit conscious of them.

We aren't going to overturn a lifetime of experience, nor would we want to. We need to start out by becoming aware of the processes that work for us, then move on to improving them step by step. What bad habits have you picked up in your decision-making? Which steps do you skip and which do you overemphasize? Do your poor decisions tend to stem from bad information, poor evaluation, incorrect calculation, or a combination of these things?

Material, the Fundamental Element

Few of us will ever lead a multinational corporation or run in a national election, but all of our routine daily decisions benefit from an improved process. The key to that is the ability to correctly assess and evaluate a situation. By becoming more aware of all the elements, all the factors in play, we train ourselves to think strategically, or as we say in chess, positionally.

Evaluating a position goes well beyond looking for the best move. The move is only the result, the product of an equation that must first be imagined and developed. So, determine the relevant factors, measure them, and, most critically, determine the optimal balance among them. Before you can begin your search for the keys to a position, you have to perform this basic due diligence. We can categorize these factors into three groups: material, time, and quality.

The simplest and perhaps most important area to evaluate is material. Assets, stock, cash, goods, pieces and pawns, it's all material. In chess, the first thing we do when we look at the board is count the pieces. How many pawns, how many knights and rooks? Do I have more or less material than my opponent?

When we first learn the game, we are all terrible materialists. We capture as many enemy pieces as we can without paying much attention to other factors. A game between two beginners can look more like Pac-Man than chess as the two competitors gobble up each other's pieces. This is a normal and healthy way to start out. Being told the values is one thing, but only experience really teaches you what those values signify in the "real world" of chess.

In other areas too, most of our objective measurements of success and failure come down to material. On a basic personal level, that means food, water, and shelter. Now that we as a society can express value electronically, it might be an account balance, or stocks or funds in banks. In warfare it's which side has more soldiers, more guns, more ships. In business it's factories, employees, stock, cash on hand.

It isn't always easy to assess the true value of material. We all have personal attachments to certain assets that have little to do with their objective value. These sentimental attachments can distort your evaluation ability considerably, if not always in a harmful way.

When I was a child, my favorite piece was the bishop, for no reason I can remember today. Even in my earliest games I was a great believer in the power of the bishop, and I avoided their exchange at all cost, a habit that often proved detrimental. Other beginners might be attracted to the unusual leaping ability of the knight or, alternatively, develop a fear of this most unpredictable piece.

A significant part of Botvinnik's intensive research of his opponents was dedicated to discovering such biases in their play. He would comb through their games looking for errors, then try to categorize them in a way he could later exploit. In his teachings Botvinnik made it clear that the worst type of mistake was one produced due to a bad habit because it made you predictable.

Our friends, colleagues, and family usually know much more about our bad habits than we do. Hearing about these psychological tics can be as surprising as being told by your spouse that you snore. Prejudices and preferences in your decisions are unlikely to be harmful as long as you are aware of them and actively work to iron them out. Awareness can mean the difference between a harmless habit and a bias that leads to a dangerous loss of objectivity.

It doesn't take long in chess or any other pursuit to realize that there is much more to life than material. The first time you are checkmated despite having a big material advantage, you've learned an important lesson. The ultimate value of the king trumps everything else on the board, and your value system begins to adjust. You realize that other factors can be even more important.

Time Is Money

Anyone who has ever worked for an hourly wage knows that in the most basic sense time has value. Your employer exchanges material—money—for labor, as measured by the hours you work. This is "clock time," measured and understood in the same way everywhere. It is quite different from what chess players call "board time," which is the number of steps it takes to accomplish an objective.

Chess players are used to thinking of both types of time during a game. Your clock is ticking and you have a limited amount of time to make all your moves: clock time. Then you have the game itself, where time is divided neatly into moves, alternating between you and your opponent. How many moves does it take to get from point A to point B? How long will it take for my knight to threaten his queen? Can I reach my objective before my opponent reaches his? That is board time. And as I hope to show, success in every kind of enterprise requires the ability to understand and use both sorts of time to your advantage.

The simplest way to demonstrate this is to look at the difference between playing white and black. White goes first, putting him a single move ahead at the start, giving him an advantage in board time. It is a matter of historical debate whether the advantage of the first move should prove enough to force a win for white if both sides play perfectly. As humans we are so far from perfect that this can never be proven. Among amateurs, who are more likely to make errors and wasteful moves, the narrow advantage of that single move at the start is rarely decisive. But among professionals, being one move ahead is a tangible plus. With precise play, that single move allows white to apply pressure and make threats against black's position. White is acting, black is reacting. Statistics bear out the value of the first move: at the Grandmaster level white wins twenty-nine percent of the time, black eighteen percent, and fifty-three percent of games are drawn. But if white takes too long to decide his moves, he can find himself rushing decisions at the end of the game to avoid defaulting—that is, he might squander his advantage in board time due to a disadvantage in clock time.

A military commander is used to thinking of time in the same way as a chess player, but in the real world things are much more dynamic. There is practically no limit to the number of "moves" you and your enemies can make at the same time. Multiple attacks and counterattacks can take place concurrently around the battlefield, or around the world. But the definition of time remains the same because in both cases what matters is how quickly an objective can be achieved, whether it be on the battlefield or the chessboard.

Time is not gained just by moving faster or by taking shortcuts. Time can often be bought or swapped for material assets. Think of it as paying extra money (material) for express delivery (time). Time for material is the first of the trade-offs in our evaluation system. When is it worth material to achieve an objective, and how much material to invest? How do we know we are getting our "material's worth" in time?

When Time Matters Most

No one understood the value of time and material better than Mikhail Tal. The first time I saw Tal in person, I was ten years old, and while his year as world champion had come and gone before I was born, his thrilling games were the favorite of every schoolboy. Tal was the ultimate "time player." When his attacking genius was in full flight, his pieces seemed to move not just better but somehow faster than his opponent's. How was this possible? The young Tal cared much less for material than most players and would happily give up almost any number of pawns and pieces in exchange for more time to bring his other forces into action against the enemy king. He constantly pushed his opponents onto the defensive, leading to errors and disaster. This sounds simple, but few have been able to imitate Tal's unique gift for knowing just how far he could go, and few would dare give up as much material as he would.

It's easy to see that when you're attacking, being a move ahead is more important than material. But how much more important? Is one move worth two pawns? Or two moves worth a bishop? There is no simple value chart for time, only case-by-case evaluation. Ask a general if he would rather have another company of men or an extra few days. During peacetime he'd rather have the men, while in a guerrilla combat situation the extra time could be much more valuable.

In chess we talk about open positions and closed positions. An open position has many clear lines for your pieces, more options to move in different directions, and more opportunities for attack and counterattack. A closed position usually means a slow, strategic maneuvering game, the chess equivalent of trench warfare. In an open game the value of a move is much greater than in a closed game because a single attack can do much more damage. If the position is blocked and there is little activity overall, there is less need for speed.

These factors occur in business as well. Imagine that you own a company that is working on a new product line. You know a competitor is working on a similar project and is at around the same stage in development. Should you rush your products to market to beat Company B? Or should you spend more money on development to try to ensure your product is superior to Company B's? Of course the answers always depend on real-world factors, so recognizing what sort of situation we are in is a crucial part of the evaluation. Before you start considering trade-offs, take a good look around. What industry are these companies in? What type of product is it? Time is always a factor, but is it really of the essence in this case, or are you just being impatient? Putting a new heart medicine on the market isn't the same as trying to get the latest gadget out in time for Christmas shoppers. What's important is recognizing the exchange between time and material.

My third world championship match with Anatoly Karpov presents a wonderfully clear example of this constant fluctuation. It was the eighth game of our 1986 match, which was split between London and Leningrad, as St. Petersburg was still known at the time. Searching for an advantage, I offered Karpov a pawn in exchange for the opportunity to attack his king, judging that the two moves I would gain against his king were worth the price of a pawn on the other side of the board.

Karpov had done the same math, and after his evaluation he captured the pawn. My attack quickly built up steam until it was Karpov's turn to offer material in order to organize a defense of his king. He exposed his rook to my bishop; taking it would give me a slight material advantage, but at the cost of abandoning my attack and allowing him to consolidate his position. This was a classic example of the fluidity in the factors of material and time as they played a role in both of our games. I gave up material for attacking time, and later Karpov offered the material back to gain time for his defense.

I declined the offer, not wanting to go from lender to borrower so quickly. (It's worth noting that Karpov, as a matter of style, would certainly have taken the material had our positions been reversed. Taking the rook guaranteed a small advantage with no risk, exactly the sort of situation Karpov enjoyed.) I ignored the rook and instead continued on, down a pawn, looking for a way to break through. A few moves later I even gave up another pawn to keep my attack alive, even though this meant I was likely to lose if my attack didn't succeed. As so often happens, an advantage in board time—pressure and threats that force your opponent to react—results in an advantage in clock time. Move after move, Karpov had to burn a lot of time finding his way through all the dangers to his king. With ten moves still to go until we got more time added to our clocks, Karpov lost on time, a nearly unprecedented event in his long career.

This game serves as a testament to my philosophy of preferring time over material, favoring dynamic factors over static factors. These evaluation preferences are part of one's style and aren't necessarily superior or inferior to those of others, only different. Karpov lost that game; does that mean he was wrong in his evaluation of the position? Or that I was right? Neither. In another situation, material might have triumphed over time. What's important here is to recognize these factors at play.

The Third Factor: Quality

Each piece in chess has a standard value that allows us to quickly add up who's ahead in the arms race. Our standard of measurement, our basic currency, is the pawn. Each player starts with eight of these foot soldiers, the most limited and least valuable members of the army. Even the word *pawn* has come to connote weakness and expendability. We even say "pawns and pieces," not including them in the same class as bishops, knights, and rooks.

Pawns provide a useful system of equivalent value. Knights and bishops are said to be worth three pawns. Rooks are five pawns, while the queen is worth nine. (The king, whose capture ends the game, is weak but priceless.) So informed, a beginner can go into battle knowing that he shouldn't give up a knight for a pawn, or a rook for a knight.

But for the experienced player, much more goes into the evaluation of a position than counting pieces and moves. The piece values fluctuate depending on your position and can change after every turn. The same is true about the value of a move, unless we believe Tal's knights really were faster. Material is the fundamental reference point; time is movement and action. To be correctly understood and utilized the two elements must be governed by a third element: quality.

Generations of platitudes teach us that there is good money and bad. There is even the entrenched notion of "quality time." In chess we talk about a weak knight or a particularly strong pawn, because their value changes depending on their placement and on other factors. A knight located in the center of the board—where it controls more territory and can join the fight in any region—is almost always more valuable than one near the edge of the board, a concept that is immortalized in the old chess maxim "A knight on the rim is dim."

On the real field of battle as well, all terrain is not equally valued. Throughout the history of warfare combatants have sought the highest ground available. From the heights your archers, and later your artillery, can shoot farther and your commanders can better see the battle develop. Satellites and airpower have changed these ancient equations in many ways, but it will always be true that where your forces are placed can be as important as their strength in numbers. Placement provides, or limits, utility, which is what the commander—or the business executive or the chess player—seeks.

What Makes a Bad Bishop Bad?

We often talk about having a "good" bishop or a "bad" bishop, and understanding how this can be provides insight into the subtle but essential differences in the materials that we work with every day. My childhood favorite, the bishop—called an elephant in Russian and a fool in French—is a good example because of the way its movement is limited. The bishop can travel as many squares as it likes in any diagonal direction, but on only one color of the board. This gives it great range but makes it predictable. If many of the squares of the bishop's color are occupied by pawns of the same color, its mobility is extremely limited.

Such a bishop is called bad, but its intrinsic nature is no different from when the game started. Its quality has been diminished by the circumstances around it. From a practical standpoint, that of utility, it is inferior and should be considered as such. If I have a bad bishop, I would be glad to trade it off for another piece.

The CEO and the general have to be alert to bad pieces in their worlds as well. When Jack Welch took over the behemoth that was General Electric in 1981, one of the first things he did was to make a list of all the divisions in the company that weren't performing up to his standards. The directors of those operations were told they had to improve or their divisions would be sold or closed down. Instead of hanging on to units solely for their presumed material value, GE would focus on what it was best at and cut back in the areas where it wasn't doing well.

Any chess master would recognize Welch's strategy as employing the principle of improving your worst piece. He was applying Tarrasch's dictum "One badly placed piece makes your whole position bad!" If you have a bad bishop, you try to find a way to activate it, to make it "good." If it can't be rehabilitated, you try to swap it off or eliminate it. The same is true of ineffective material in any business or enterprise. Put that bad piece, that underperforming asset, to good use or get rid of it and your overall position will improve.

Returning to our stock portfolios, we can see why the same strategies don't always apply. Any good investment counselor will tell you to keep a balanced portfolio with a mix of risky and stable assets depending on your age, needs, and income. If you constantly sell the things that aren't performing well at the moment, you will inevitably be out of position at some point—and it could happen at a crucial juncture when you have everything to lose.

Putting the Elements into Action

Only in extreme cases can material in chess be completely inert and worthless. A knight that is trapped in the corner may someday escape and play a critical role in the fight. One of the difficulties programmers have in improving computer chess programs is the "concept of never" and how it relates to the value of material. Even a weak human player can see that a piece has permanently been trapped and is therefore worthless. But to a computer that piece still has the same numeric value in its calculations as before it was trapped. Perhaps some points are deducted for loss of mobility, but there is no good way to teach a computer that a bishop on square X is worth three pawns but on square Y it's only worth one.

This gives us different classes of material: long-term and dynamic. Investment portfolios work much the same way. Depending on personal style and needs, your portfolio might be full of dynamic (liquid) assets, which require constant attention and reassessment. Or the portfolio might be aimed at long-term growth and preservation of capital (bonds) for a retirement that is still decades off. My play in the aforementioned game with Karpov showed my preference for dynamism and his for the long term. I sacrificed pawns to make my remaining material more valuable in the short run. Had my attack failed, his investment in long-term material advantages would have won the day.

This was a typical theme of many of my games against Karpov thanks to our different natures regarding time and material. In our first world championship match my skills were not so well developed, and Karpov's material advantage deflected my attacks. His evaluations were superior. But by the London match, a year and a half later, I had learned to be less rash with giving away material, and it was a different story.

Double-Edged Evaluation

"Who is winning?" is a simple enough question, but real evaluation is a complex undertaking. First we count material. If one player has a

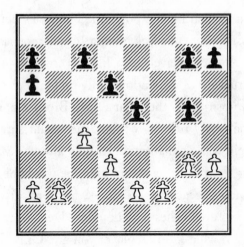

significant advantage here, we can say he is winning unless his opponent has compensation in time and/or quality. Whose forces are better developed and placed more aggressively? How quickly can one side attack and the other defend? How long will it take for reinforcements to arrive? Who commands more territory? Is someone's king in danger? These are all qualitative evaluations, and each carries a different degree of significance.

One way to illustrate the relative nature of qualitative evaluations—the type that leaders in every enterprise must do each day—is to examine the qualities of a group of pawns on a chessboard. A chess visual aid will help us here (you don't even need to know how to move the pieces).

Take a look at the difference between the white and black pawns in the diagram. Both sides have the full contingent of eight, so they are equal in material. The qualitative difference here is structure, the form the pawns take as a group. White's are orderly and form a complete wall across the board. Black's are fragmented into three "islands." In two cases, one black pawn stands in front of another, limiting its mobility. Thus we would say that white has a "superior pawn structure."

In that we would be correct, and the game would be simple if there were no pieces or kings. But in a real game, the pawn structure would be just one factor in evaluating the position. The holes between the black pawns could possibly benefit black, giving him compensation for his inferior structure. A chess player who likes long-term static advantages such as a solid structure would undoubtedly prefer to play the white side. But show such a position to the great David Bronstein, who challenged Botvinnik for the world title in 1951, and he would surely prefer black! Like me, Bronstein was a dynamic player who always favored short-term activity over long-term considerations. Here he would be content to have those structural holes because he would use them to activate his pieces. I tend to look at structure in chess as a double-edged sword; it can cut both ways, depending on what kind of player you are. Only the truly accomplished strategist will be able to see how—and why—the concept of structure works this way in the situations he faces every day.

Finer, double-edged factors such as structure come into focus only when the forces are evenly matched in the essential areas. The stronger the players, and the more balanced the game, the more the evaluation comes down to the tiniest details. While major differences in material and time are relatively obvious, distinctions in these more subtle criteria only show under great pressure, and it is the mark of a great player to be able to detect and exploit them. The saying goes that the "devil is in the details," and these secondary factors are the chess player's devils. Any police officer can follow a thief's footsteps in the snow, but Sherlock Holmes could deduce an amazing amount from clues invisible to others.

Personal Return on Investment

What are the smaller issues that can have a big impact on our lives? Few of us need to worry about food and water, yet we obsess over material things as much as our ancestors. The higher concepts of utility, quality, and happiness sound too vague and philosophical to think about. We think about time as something not to waste, not as something to invest.

Our pursuit of education provides an elegant rebuttal to that idea. What is going to college if not an investment of material and time for quality? We give time and money to gain skills that will raise our intrinsic value to an employer. Higher education is one way we (or our parents) make material sacrifices to increase the quality of our position in the future. The more we can afford to invest, the greater our return will be. If you have the money and grades to go to a top university, you will be able to gain a superior education, make better contacts, and be better positioned to enter the job market.

Perhaps a more openly mercenary path, getting an MBA, offers a clearer example. An executive making a hundred thousand dollars a year decides to leave a good job and spend tens or hundreds of thousands of dollars to go back to school. By all accounts, going to business school isn't much fun, so short-term enjoyment isn't a motive. Considering the investment of time and material, the qualitative return must be judged to be high since business school enrollments continue to rise.

That return in quality comes in the shape of skills and contacts, which then lead to a better job. Higher pay and more responsibility enhance the new MBA's quality of life, or at least that's the way the formula is supposed to work. Certainly, many people with business degrees are unhappy. A new high-paying job might take up so much time that none is left for activities that are significant components of happiness. The difficulty is in being aware of these small factors and evaluating them before we make a decision that affects them.

The questions we must ask are not only about trade-offs. Giving up material doesn't always result in a gain of time, or vice versa. At least in chess, you can have it all or lose it all. The player with a winning position will usually have more pieces *and* be ahead in time *and* have superior placement and position. Consider this the "rich grow richer" variation.

A politician on the campaign trail is seeking happiness by way of winning the election. The candidate has a limited amount of time and a limited amount of money. His strategy is predicated on using these things to give the biggest possible boost to his image in the eyes of the electorate. Although a huge amount of money is spent on campaigns, now more than ever, experience shows that subtle elements can still surprise. A single sound bite or gaffe can shift perception dramatically, for better or for worse. Dan Quayle's mangling of the spelling of the word *potato* in front of a classroom full of kids while on the campaign trail mangled his political career forever. However, such things only rarely overcome more fundamental advantages and disadvantages.

MTQ on the Home Front

These exchanges between material, time, and quality are just as powerful in our personal lives. For example, my wife, Dasha, and I recently bought a new home, an ordeal that for me involved no fewer considerations—and no less stress—than playing in a world championship match. Anyone who has bought a home or even rented an apartment knows how many trade-offs are involved. They go well beyond the obvious one of material vs. quality. Even if you believe that "you get what you pay for" and the more you pay the better house you'll get, figuring out precisely what "better" means is complex, especially if you have a family, which increases the number of decisions and the number of decision-makers.

The same cliché rules in both real estate and chess: "location, location, location." Where you live is as important as what you live in. If you have children, you'll want to be near a school; if you work long hours, you'll want to be near your office. In any case, you'll want a neighborhood that's safe, convenient to shopping and entertainment, and so on. These are the obvious qualities people look for. We have equivalent guidelines in chess too. "Play in the center." "Get your king to safety quickly." These rules of thumb serve as useful guides for beginners. But as players advance, they begin to detect the occasional exceptions to the rules, and capitalizing on these exceptions is what separates a great player from a good one.

There is no universal formula for evaluation. We get caught up in standardized rhetoric and end up with something that doesn't fit our unique needs. For the most part we all know what we like and make decisions accordingly, but under pressure we can easily be confused and lose sight of our goals. The little things are hard to keep in mind when there are so many big things, so it's no surprise that the "small stuff" causes the most problems.

Many fail by overdependence on the areas they best understand. It is comforting to stick to what you know, and you are often unaware that a problem can be seen from a different perspective. If you are so focused on just one aspect of a situation—if you fall blindly in love with your bishops, or that corner office, or that big tree in the backyard—you will almost certainly make mistakes in your evaluation.

While you can "have it all" in chess, and perhaps even in life, that elysian condition is not useful for learning. Most of the time we will have to balance, exchange, and evaluate over and over. If we do this well enough to blend material, time, and quality into a multidimensional evaluation, we gain a clear idea of what we want and can then plan on how to achieve it. When we see all the factors, we can then learn how to shift them and build them. Without expanding our powers of evaluation we risk fulfilling Oscar Wilde's famous observation about knowing "the price of everything and the value of nothing."

Material is only as valuable as the use it can be put to. Time for action is only important if it helps us make our material more useful. Most people would welcome having an extra hour in the day, but not the man in a jail cell. The message here is, use time to improve your material, not just acquire more of it. Material for its own sake is as useless as wasted time in the pursuit of our goals.

Useful material and well-spent time lead to winning in a chess game. In the corporate world they lead to higher revenues. In war and politics they lead to victory. And I might add that in everyday life, "victory" can simplistically, perhaps a little romantically, be defined as happiness. Money can't buy it, after all. But I believe that by using your time wisely you can put all your material to your best advantage and achieve the ultimate goal of quality. That's the promise of the material-time-quality concept—in chess and in life.

CHAPTER 8

EXCHANGES AND IMBALANCES

Freezing the Game

An imbalance is any lack of symmetry that can be exploited to one's advantage. In chess this refers to the quantitative and qualitative differences between your opponent's forces and your own. A game may appear to be deadlocked, but when you play like a master and diligently consider all three MTQ factors, imbalances always exist because even if the pieces are completely symmetrical on the board, it is always someone's turn. The player whose move it is has an advantage in time, which breaks the balance.

Suspending the game in time is a useful way to teach students how to evaluate qualitative factors such as structure and space. We do this by showing a chess position without revealing whose move it is. At first this sounds preposterous. If the entire purpose is to decide the best move, isn't it essential to know whose move it is? The purpose of this technique is precisely to remove the anxiety about choosing the next move and to encourage the player to appreciate the subtle elements in play across the board without prejudice. This technique taught students to better consider the various destinations and to evaluate them thoroughly instead of focusing on where to go. In real play the students immediately start making suggestions for the next move, trying one after another without thinking things through, and they tend to miss the big picture and the strategic possibilities that are present at each move. I experienced a similar syndrome when I ventured into the business of the Internet.

In 1999, my partners and I were getting ready to launch a giant Internet chess portal bearing my name. As the site neared completion, the designers worked with testers and focus groups to see how well the design and navigation worked in practice. It was tragicomic to watch the testers completely ignore the signs and instructions that had carefully been worked out by my team and me and deliberately placed by the Web designers. Instead, following what the experts told me is the normal pattern, the users would immediately click on whatever caught their eye and, if unhappy with the result, jump back and try again, or they'd go off in a totally different direction. They ignored most of the menu choices we had worked so hard to perfect. The desire to be quick and to keep moving forward drove them.

Unfortunately, this reflects how many of us go about making decisions all the time. We take our best guess and plunge forward, barely considering the options before us. There is a huge difference between just browsing the possible moves and evaluating the situation. Frequently our intuitive leaps prove fruitful, and for at least a short time we get what we want and need. But my years as a chess player have taught me how important it is to do the analysis that will clearly show you which of the options is superior. Instinctive evaluation is better than none at all, but we can't confuse it with understanding even if the results aren't always bad.

For example, getting back to those beginning chess students, what if one of them, through intuition or luck or both, hurriedly calls out the right move when presented with a position to analyze? It's to his credit, but it doesn't mean he really understands the position, and it may lead to the formation of bad habits. Only a deliberate analysis leads us to the core of the position. This in turn narrows our options and informs our decisions. That's when we reintroduce the time factor and use our evaluation to decide on the best move.

This isolation technique is utilized in business schools to train students in various methods of evaluating a company or a case study. To start out, the class might be given only a balance sheet with no knowledge of the competition, perhaps even of the industry. Or they might be shown only the market share of the company's products relative to the competition. Introducing elements one by one attempts to eliminate gaps in education and evaluation habits. When students have the full picture, they can see how all the elements combine to form a single, unique image.

Once we have frozen play, we still have to know what to analyze and how to weigh that analysis. On a chessboard, the number of factors to consider is limited, but the number of ways to consider them is unlimited. As we discussed earlier, even strong players will differ over the relative importance of the different elements. The simplest test is to present a position and ask someone which side he would prefer to play. White or black? Who is better and why? The position may be equal, but a human being is a creature of preference and can never be completely objective. Being aware of your preferences and prejudices can be as critical as how well you observe the external factors.

We can move our theoretical chess position to the military battlefield or the corporate boardroom. Before a general launches an attack he evaluates as many factors as he can. He must consider terrain, weather, force readiness, supply lines, political support, and dozens of other things before he makes his move. Successful companies focus on long-term goals established by accurate evaluation. A CEO can't be ruled by a perceived need to respond immediately to every move the competition makes or he won't have any real strategy of his own.

The Search for Compensation

A proper evaluation is a search for advantage or compensation for disadvantage. Few advantages are unconditional, and most disadvantages—like clouds—come with a silver lining. Tarrasch was exaggerating only slightly when he wrote, "Every move creates a weakness." Unless a move delivers checkmate, it has negatives as well as positives. The same is true of static characteristics. For example, when your pawns advance, you gain space to maneuver your pieces, but at the expense of weakening your defenses. When troops advance, lines of communication and supply can be cut or become disorganized.

Material losses are typically the only purely negative factor, although in extreme cases you might benefit by losing a member of your own forces. If an army's fast-moving cavalry is hemmed in by its own foot soldiers, a general can't just sacrifice his slower-moving troops. But in chess it's not uncommon to play a "clearance sacrifice" by throwing a pawn into the teeth of the enemy to clear the lines for your pieces to advance.

If an asset is nearly worthless and has no prospects of improvement, you might as well get what you can for it while you can. Amateurs who dabble in the stock market are famous for holding on to losing stocks all the way to the bottom, imagining that they haven't really lost anything until they've sold, which is a self-destructive fallacy. The cold-blooded investor knows that getting something now is better than nothing later.

At a tournament in Yugoslavia in 1983 I had the opportunity to dispose of some falling shares in the form of a bishop. In my game against the leading Hungarian player, Lajos Portisch, I was straining to find a way to exploit my slight lead in development. I wanted to use this dynamic advantage to launch an attack on his king. The problem was, all of my pieces needed to use the same central square. If I played my knight there, it would block my bishop, cutting it out of the game entirely. This led me to wonder—if the bishop wasn't participating actively at this exact moment in the game, why couldn't I exchange it for something of value in the black position, such as the pawn right in front of the black king?

Giving up a bishop for a single pawn doesn't make any sense from a material perspective, but I had the initiative—an advantage in board time—and it was more time I needed. That is, my pieces were close to reaching key targets before my opponent could defend them. With a little more speed they would crash home with decisive effect. To gain that board time I invested more material. The bishop would otherwise be unemployed in my planned operation, and this way it could be sacrificed to further increase my dynamic advantage. I gave up the bishop, and with his king exposed, Portisch had to lose more time running for cover. Eventually my activity overwhelmed his material lead.

In chess as in life we total up the pluses and minuses in a position, then go to work figuring out how to improve our side of the ledger. We want to create weaknesses in our opponent's camp while strengthening our own. Essential to this is turning our weaknesses into strengths, or at least minimizing them. A theoretical weakness, a by-the-book disadvantage, that can't be exploited by your opponent is really not a weakness at all.

Successfully exploiting your advantages leads to greater advantages, eventually great enough to win a decisive amount of material. This is where the alchemy comes in, the transformation of one type of advantage into another. With accurate play we can turn material into time and back again, or invest both for a high return in quality.

The Laws of Thermodynamics, Chess, and Quality of Life

The first law of thermodynamics tells us that the total amount of energy in a system is constant, that if we move energy into one area, we lose an equal amount from another. To put it another way, energy can't spontaneously be created or destroyed, only transferred from one place to another or transmuted from one form into another.

On the chessboard we try to break that law—to create both energy and material. If a pawn reaches the other side of the board, it can be "promoted" into any piece, even another queen. (Of course you can't have another king. In chess, bigamy is acceptable but monarchy is absolute.) That way we improve—we add to—the energy of our own pieces. Of course in a typical game of attack and counterattack, our opponent does the same thing, marshaling his forces and increasing his activity level, which is what makes the game dynamic.

If done right, each chessboard transformation increases the quality of our position. In exchange for time—say two moves—I can bring my knight over to a superior location, and in so doing I've increased that knight's energy, his power to do harm. Or when I sacrifice a pawn, my opponent has to lose a move or two to capture it, giving me time to augment my attack. Again, the material-time-quality concept forms the basic law of chess.

A company can—and should—view its own playing field in a similar way. An advantage in cash reserves—material—is turned into research on new products, or employee bonuses, or more advertising, or a modernized factory. Looking at the assets of your competitors enables you to find imbalances you can exploit. Even if your opponent dominates in many areas, you can try to develop a positive imbalance of your own—and displace some energy. If we can detect or cultivate a weak spot in our opponent's position, we can then attempt to transform our position to take advantage of that weakness. Here's an example from the world of technology.

Strategy on the Browser Battlefield

The expression *browser war* was in wide use in the late nineties, when Netscape and Microsoft were battling for Web market share. Netscape

Navigator was first and also best; Microsoft Explorer lagged way behind in just about every respect. Its early versions were mediocre, and Navigator had a large and loyal customer base.

In response, Microsoft developed a masterful strategy of exchanges. It had negative qualitative imbalances in product quality, user base, and brand recognition. But this war wasn't just browser versus browser, it was company versus company, and here Microsoft had some positive imbalances against Netscape. First, it had a massive material advantage in cold, hard cash thanks to the success of its office suites and operating-system software. Second, Microsoft had a placement advantage; it could bundle Explorer with its other popular software. If you bought Windows or MS Office, the Microsoft browser came installed on your computer.

Microsoft didn't just give the browser away with other software. Leveraging its massive amount of cash, it simply gave it away to everybody free. This was a brutally efficient exchange of material for positional quality, and it worked wonderfully. To be fair, they also invested a lot of money into improving the quality of the Explorer browser, but that wasn't the most important factor in the race with Navigator. The much smaller Netscape saw what was going on and tried to keep up. They also cried foul and went to the courts to try to stop or at least slow Microsoft's appropriation of their energy in the browser wars. But such a small company couldn't afford to give its main product to everyone for free and still maintain quality. Netscape's attempts to bundle Navigator with other software were futile in the face of the ninety-five percent desktop dominance of Windows. Within two years Microsoft went from less than a ten percent share of the browser market to over eighty percent. They continued to gain until Netscape—and all the other competition—was entirely marginalized.

Microsoft exploited its overwhelming advantage in resources. In American Civil War terms, it played General Grant to the rest of the software world's General Lee. The Union's Grant wasn't the most brilliant tactician, but he knew he would eventually wear down the Southern army by sheer weight of troops and supplies. A war of attrition suited Grant—if not his men—just fine, and he had the brutally pragmatic nature needed to win such a war. With some stretching, we can even make an analogy to the Cold War. By constantly increasing military spending the USA eventually bankrupted the USSR, which couldn't keep up the pace of spending. Although in this case the Communist side also suffered from the fatal "bug" of a bankrupt ideology.

All Change Comes at a Cost

When measuring imbalances, you should consider the elements of your operation not just in relation to your rivals', but also in relation to one another. In chess we talk about having harmony in our position. Are your pieces working together? Is your material developed in accordance with your strategic goals? The difficulty of achieving successful coordination increases with the number of assets. The corporate megamergers of the past decade illustrate this well. Time Warner and AOL came together in a deal of record proportions in 2001, and investors are now considering separating the companies again. Bigger isn't always better, especially if it comes at the cost of coordination.

The chess bishop can move only diagonally, meaning each bishop spends its entire life on the squares of one color, white or black. Each player starts the game with two bishops, and the "bishop pair" can attack or defend any square on the board. When they work side by side, two bishops can be a devastating attacking force. This is why when one bishop is captured, often the other is greatly diminished as well. The remaining bishop can target only half the squares on the board, so your opponent knows he is safe on those squares, at least from the bishop. The combined power of the bishop pair is far greater than the sum of its parts. Similarly, two companies might combine to be worth far more than they were before if they can work together in harmony. Or, as in the case of Time Warner and AOL, they might turn out to be worth less because of conflicts.

Overextending Our Reach

Physics also tells us that "ordered systems lose less energy than chaotic systems." In chess terms, when our pieces work together, they can turn one advantage into another without losing quality. A position or a company or a military unit that is disorganized can be torn apart by attempting a transformation. Trying to achieve the objective can leave them so depleted that they are quickly wiped out. This happens most frequently—in chess and in life—when positions or circumstances are already tenuous.

The phrase *hastening defeat* appears frequently in the annotation of chess games. A player in a difficult position tends to make mistakes due to the psychological pressure that comes with knowing he's in trouble. But another key dynamic is also at work: an inferior position is less able to withstand the loss of energy required by an attempt at change. This is why a company that is in financial trouble should never gamble on a risky venture. Without stability that risky venture could lead to the total collapse of the company—even if the gamble succeeds in its immediate objectives.

Businesses too hasten defeat by overextending themselves. In the early 1970s, Pan Am airlines found itself in a difficult position. The global energy crisis of 1973 came right on the heels of a court battle that awarded important international routes to the company's competitors. Once dominant, Pan Am was now in grave trouble.

Pan Am tried to solve some of its problems with the purchase of a domestic airline, but, as so often happens, a bold move from a position of weakness was severely punished. They overpaid for National Airlines and accumulated huge debt. They held on by selling assets and routes, expending their material resources and hoping for a favorable change in conditions. The company was so fragile that all it would take was one more negative development to knock it out. In 1988 the Lockerbie terrorist bombing of Pan Am Flight 103 was the proverbial last straw. Bookings plummeted, and a further overall fall in air travel thanks to the first Gulf War led the company to declare bankruptcy in 1991.

The first airline giant undoubtedly had more than its fair share of bad luck, but the directors of Pan Am also suffered from their own mistakes and made themselves much more vulnerable to bad luck by overextending their material and by not taking care of the imbalances in their own position. They didn't develop domestic routes, they had a weak cash reserve, they had pending court cases. This analysis is not meant to serve as a recommendation to be conservative or to plan only for the worst-case scenario. Risk-taking is essential in any endeavor. It's the context of that risk that is so critical. If you are sensitive to your vulnerabilities and negative imbalances, you can factor them into your strategy. One imbalance is rarely decisive. You must be able to see when a confluence is forming and whether it is in your favor.

In 1993, I committed the dreadful mistake of launching an attack from a position of weakness. This wasn't at the chessboard, however, but in chess politics. Ever since the international chess federation, FIDE, had interrupted my first world championship match in 1985, I had feuded with their leadership almost without pause. In the run-up to my 1993 world championship match with Nigel Short, the Englishman called me with a tempting offer: to launch our own Professional Chess Association and play the match outside of FIDE. Here at last was a chance to break away from the corrupt bureaucracy and introduce chess into the world of modern sport.

Short was the first Western challenger for the world title since

Bobby Fischer in 1972. With his involvement I thought we could generate tremendous interest and rally the world's Grandmasters against FIDE. Just a few years before, I had created another professional players' union, but it had foundered when the Western GMs formed an opposition bloc. Suddenly here was Nigel, the last president of the Grandmaster Association, offering to join forces. Now, I thought, we could really unite the chess world. This turned out to be a terrible blunder, the worst of my career. After we made our announcement, it quickly became apparent that I had misjudged the situation. Short had no such support. I had overextended. Suddenly we were on our own and were immediately portrayed as "renegades" and "hijackers of the world championship." FIDE essentially excommunicated both of us and held an alternative world championship match parallel to the one Short and I played in London. Thus began a schism in the chess world that has never properly healed. I was so eager to achieve my goal that I was oblivious to how unlikely the plan was to succeed. I failed to correctly evaluate my position and in so doing ignored several fatal imbalances.

There are imbalances in our daily lives and we constantly struggle to transform them positively. Gaining control means finding the most favorable balance and working constantly to make positive exchanges. Norman Mailer wrote that at every moment we are either "living a little more or dying a little bit." There is no standing still, no maintaining a perfect equilibrium. We can, however, in effect freeze time by pausing for a moment in our constant search for what to do next and instead calmly evaluate the pluses and minuses. We can flout the laws of thermodynamics to create energy and quality—value and power—through positive transformations.

CHAPTER 9

PHASES OF THE GAME

Before the endgame, the gods have placed the middle game.
—SIEGBERT TARRASCH

Abraham Lincoln began his famous "House Divided" speech in 1858 with a brilliant observation: "If we could first know where we are going and whither we are tending, we could better judge what to do and how to do it." Lincoln might have added that it's worth knowing not only where you are going, but where you are. Planning and innovation both require solid grounding in the present. We can know "whither we are tending" only when we know where we are.

Over the centuries, countless methods have been developed to explain the game of chess to students and help them to better understand the path they are on in each game they play. One of the most durable methods is to break the game into three parts, or phases: the opening, the middle game, and the endgame. There is no agreed-upon formula for determining exactly when one ends and another begins, but without question each phase has distinctive characteristics and each poses problems that benefit from different modes of thinking.

Know Why We Make Each Move We Make

Simply put, the opening is the phase of the game where the battle lines are drawn. The pawns establish the contours of structure, the pieces get off the back rank and take up hostile or defensive positions. The opening, though, is far more than a trivial mobilization of forces. It establishes what sort of battle is to come and is the first and best opportunity to move the game into channels where you are better equipped to fight than your opponent. The opening is the subtlest, most difficult phase of the game, especially at the highest level of competition.

An essential element of this starting phase is the actual *opening*—the term we use to describe the hundreds of predetermined sequences of moves—the set plays, if you will—that great chess players have devised to begin games. These usually have names, such as the aforementioned Dragon variation. These proper names can derive from the player who coined the variation, the city or country where the originating game was played, or a literal—or poetic—description of the position. The Dragon variation is said to get its name for the way the alignment of the pawns looks like the constellation Draco. The names of the openings make up much of chess players' jargon, populating our discussions with everything from the Sicilian Dragon to the Maroczy Bind, from the Marshall Attack to the King's Indian.

Players, even club amateurs, dedicate hours to studying and memorizing the lines of their preferred openings. This knowledge is invaluable, but it can also be a trap. Many make the mistake of believing that if they know what a famous Grandmaster played in this exact position back in 1962, they don't have to think for themselves. The theory is this: if they can just follow the games of great players, move by move, for as as long as they can, and if they remember more than their opponent, he'll eventually make a mistake.

In competitive play, though, that theory rarely holds up. Long before a player becomes a master, he realizes that rote memorization, however prodigious, is useless without understanding. At some point, he'll reach the end of his memory's rope and be without a premade fix in a position he doesn't really understand. Without knowing *why* all the moves were made, he'll have little idea of how to continue when play inevitably advances beyond the moves he was able to store in his memory.

In June 2005 in New York I gave a special training session to a group of the leading young players in the United States. I had asked them each to bring two of their games for us to review, one win and one loss. A talented twelve-year-old raced through the opening moves of his loss, eager to get to the point where he thought he'd gone wrong. I stopped him and asked why he had played a certain pawn push in the sharp opening variation. His answer didn't surprise me: "That's what Vallejo played!" Of course I also knew that the Spanish Grandmaster had employed this move in a recent game, but I also knew that if this youngster didn't understand the motive behind the move, he was already headed for trouble.

This boy's response took me back to my own sessions with Botvinnik thirty years earlier. On more than one occasion he chided me for committing this same sin of blind emulation. The great teacher insisted that his students recognize the rationale behind every move. As a result, all of us learned to become great skeptics, even of the moves of the best players. We would discover a powerful idea behind each Grandmaster move, but we also found improvements. We studied, we questioned, we grappled with the idea behind a series of moves, and eventually we could build our understanding and create more and better strategies.

For players who depend on memorization, the opening ends when their memory runs out of moves and they have to start thinking for themselves. A rote opening might carry you to move five, or even move thirty, but this practice always inhibits your development as a player. It is one thing for a world-class player to rely on memorization; he already knows all of the whys behind the moves. For your own development it's far more important to think for yourself from the very start.

The purpose of the opening isn't just to survive the beginning of the game, it's to set the stage for the type of middle game you want—or the type of game your opponent doesn't want. To know what this is requires preparation, study, and opposition research. Which openings does tomorrow's opponent play? What happened the last few times you played each other? Can you find a new idea in one of these openings that might give you an early advantage? What types of position does he dislike? Which opening choice can lead you into those positions? If you make the right decisions at the outset, you can narrow the field of view and begin unfolding your strategy with care and precision.

Creativity in the opening phase is now most often cultivated in the comfort of home instead of in the fires of competition. Computer databases contain almost every serious game ever played, including, thanks to the Internet, those played just yesterday. You can call up your opponent's entire career in a second and look for tendencies, weaknesses, holes in his opening repertoire. Then you head to the board to face someone who has done exactly the same research on you.

By the time a player becomes a Grandmaster, almost all of his training time is dedicated to work on this first phase. The opening is the only phase that holds out the potential for true creativity and doing something entirely new. For finding something that no one else has found. Although the area narrows each year, there remains a great deal of unexplored territory. You can set off on your own without anyone knowing what you are working on. You can look for traps and new ideas and then return from your explorations ready to spring them on your opponents. It's as exciting as being an inventor in a laboratory, trying out ideas in the privacy of your own creative space. Who among us wouldn't agree that he is at his most imaginative when he is away from the office or his regular place of work? With so much precedent and history available at anyone's fingertips, the power of surprise is more difficult to harness, but it also packs a greater punch when you do find something new. So dedicate yourself to making the time, finding a space in which you can think and learn, and finding new ideas with which to shock your adversaries.

Art Is Born from Creative Conflict

It's generally agreed that the opening phase is over when the pieces have left their starting squares and the king has castled out of the center to safety. Now we come to the middle game, in which the forces become engaged. The pieces have been developed, the kings are safe (or, for more excitement, are not), and the battle lines have been drawn. It's time for the forces to meet and for blood to be spilled. It is a time for creativity, fantasy, and energy. At the start of the game the pieces are inert. The opening coils the spring, putting the pieces in position to release their energies. In the middle game come the explosions.

It is rare to be exactly where you want to be after the opening phase has ended, and it's almost impossible for both players to be happy. Your opponent is always countering, interfering with your plans, and vice versa. This means fresh evaluations are always required. You must constantly process new reports from the front. Even if you have been in this exact position in another game, it is critical to evaluate it anew, especially since your opponent is also aware you've been here before and may have prepared something nasty. The thing that worked last time may not work this time, precisely because it worked last time. Survey the landscape, examine the imbalances, and formulate a strategy.

Our MTQ analysis is similar to what those in the corporate world call SWOT reports, which stands for Strengths, Weaknesses, Opportunities, Threats. The difference in chess is that your opponent's every move, decision, and action is right there before you, all the time. Still, you must simultaneously analyze both positions—his and yours—before you can formulate and execute your strategy. You must also be aware of any immediate need for action. Do you need to put deeper strategic concerns on hold and respond to imminent danger? Can you create a threat that will force your opponent on the defensive and out of his game plan? If there aren't any immediate tactical considerations, you can continue developing your strategy and pushing toward your intermediate objectives—the process you began in the opening.

All of the elements that elevate chess to an art are native to the middle game. Poor opening research can be overcome by tactical brilliance. Deep calculations can operate in harmony with daring visions. Total disaster lurks around every corner as the dynamic force of the pieces is maximized. Battlefield commanders take over from armchair generals. More than anything, the middle game rewards action over reaction. It is the attacking phase, and the fight for the initiative is paramount.

The middle game requires alertness in general and alertness to patterns in particular. These are general ideas that anyone can learn with practice; the more you play, the better you become at recognizing the patterns and applying the solutions. That is, to find similarities to positions you have seen before and then to recall what worked (or what didn't work) in that situation. There is still potential for great creativity, if you are able to relate known patterns to new positions to find the unique solution: the best move.

In the business world, for example, a company enters the middle game as soon as a product is launched into the market. Preparation is over and now it's time to maneuver with advertising and price points. How is this product similar to previous ones? How is it different? What has worked before and how can this campaign improve on past efforts? Every decision in this phase is largely based on our ability to find parallels. The touch of genius comes in extending them beyond what others believed possible.

What little concrete study of the middle game there is comes from its evolution from the opening, one of the key transition points. The opening serves only to establish the outlines of the middle game, so it can be useful, even essential, to push your study of the opening phase into the "real world" of middle-game action. This is why it is so important to study complete chess games, not just look at the opening moves. This is also why business schools have largely switched to the case-study method instead of focusing on theory. All the study and preparation in the world can't show you what it's really going to be like in the wild. Observing typical plans in action, mistakes and accidents included, is vastly superior to ivory-tower planning.

Make Sure a Good Peace Follows a Good War

Much beloved by writers, politicians, and businesspeople as a metaphor, the endgame is simply the result of piece exchanges. When the dynamic potential of the armies has diminished to a minimal level, the middle game has ended. The energy and tension of the middle game with all its elements of surprise, attack, and defense give way to a technical phase. When only the last few survivors remain on the battlefield, raw logic and calculation take over. And then we are in the endgame.

There is still a great deal of uncharted territory in the opening phase of the game. New ideas, new concepts, new plans in old and forgotten variations, there is still much to discover in the opening. The tactical patterns and strategic concepts of the middle game have been well mapped out by generations of Grandmasters, although there are occasional fresh twists. In the endgame, however, the plans and possibilities are open and known to all, an almost mathematical exercise. This isn't to say that everything is predetermined. With flawless play from both sides, the endgame will advance toward a predictable conclusion. But since humans are flawed, damage can be inflicted or repaired. Even if one player is at a clear disadvantage, he may simply outplay his opponent.

The endgame represents the treaty negotiations after the fighting has ended. The masterful French diplomat Talleyrand pulled off just such an endgame coup at the Congress of Vienna in 1814–15. France went into the conference with low hopes. After its defeat in the Napoleonic Wars, it was a disgraced and occupied nation that could expect to have little influence at the congress that would reshape Europe. And yet the wily Talleyrand (having craftily maneuvered to have Napoleon removed from power) managed to divide the conquering allies and create new alliances that preserved most of France's territorial boundaries. France had entered the negotiating phase, the endgame after the wars, with a losing position. But with almost nothing in MTQ assets at his disposal, by skillful maneuvering Talleyrand changed the fate of Europe.

The opposite course is also possible, sadly. Few things are more tragic than playing a strong opening, a brilliant middle-game attack, then having the win evaporate with one wrong move in the endgame. This happened to me on no less a stage than my world championship match against Nigel Short in London, 1993.

In a fierce opening duel I confronted a new opening idea Nigel had introduced earlier in the match. I got a significant edge out of the opening and in the middle game successfully resisted his attempts to get things back on track. I brought a material advantage into the endgame. The game had simplified down to just one rook for my opponent and a rook and two pawns for me. (We don't count the kings as they are always on the board.) It was a winning position and I was only waiting for Short to resign—that was my first mistake. We were both on autopilot for the final moves, and not until after the game did someone point out we had both blundered horribly near the end. Even with just two pawns and two rooks on the board I had made a slip, playing a "natural" move with my pawn that permitted Short a defensive maneuver that would allow him to draw the game. But Short, also blind to the opportunity, responded with his own "natural" move. He resigned a half dozen moves later.

How could the world champion and his challenger both miss something so important in the endgame despite having so few pieces on the board to create complications? I think it's because the aridity of the endgame, its lack of dynamism, leads players to become blind to opportunity. The technical phase can be boring because there is little opportunity for creativity, for art. Boredom leads to complacency and mistakes.

The same is true in the workplace. If one is faced with a repetitive job, it can be difficult to stay alert to opportunities to solve problems creatively. Your instincts slowly go numb when every analysis returns the same answers over and over. What should be a search for excellence and the best solution eventually turns into a "good enough" mentality. We must strive to keep things fresh so we can rely on and enhance our instincts instead of falling into mental ruts. General Electric's Jack Welch once sent the senior manager of an underperforming GE sector on a month's vacation so he could come back and "act as though you hadn't been running it for four years." Many companies regularly rotate managers or have programs where top executives drop in on other areas so problems can be seen through fresh eyes. If we don't stay sharp, the edges begin to blur, and subtle differences fall through the cracks, differences that can be critically important at decisive moments.

Endgame play is typically seen as binary: good or bad, with little room for style. But the best endgame players find inspiration in the details, in the precision it takes to complete a successful move at a time when the field of battle presents few options. Cautious, patient, and calculating players excel in the endgame. Petrosian and Karpov, for example, were better in this phase of the game than Spassky and I. Attackers who thrive on the dynamism of the middle game and the creative aspects of the opening often find a natural enemy in the sterile endgame.

Eliminating Phase Bias

Of course the best players in history had to excel at every phase of the game to reach the top. There is, however, still room to shine in certain areas. I freely confess that my endgame prowess fell short of my middle-game skills and my opening play. Karpov was stronger in the middle and final phases than he was in the opening, although he compensated by working with well-chosen coaches.

Vladimir Kramnik, who took my title in 2000, has excellent opening preparation, and he shines in the endgame as well. In the dynamic middle game, but only relative to his play in the opening and the endgame, the quality of his play lacks consistency.

It's a good exercise to break down your own skills and performances this way. What are your strong points? Creative preparation? Fluid action? Calculating details? Do you shy away from any of these areas? Many players depend too heavily on a talent for one area or another, which limits their growth and their success. A tenable endgame is better than an inferior middle game, but if you don't like quiet positions, you may not realize this until it is too late. You must work to discover and eliminate the weaker parts of your game.

For me this has always meant controlling my desire for action and stopping to consider when it might be counterproductive. My love of dynamic complications often led me to avoid simplicity when perhaps it was the wisest choice. This inclination was strong in me even away from the chessboard, where my instincts were usually correct. My years working to overcome this tendency in my chess has helped me in my transition to politics. I am quicker to realize when it's time to stop attacking and to begin maneuvering and negotiating.

Don't Bring a Knife to a Gunfight

One phase often changes to another invisibly—and sometimes changes back with as little notice. What is important is to not make assumptions about a position that depend too much on the characteristics of a single phase. What works to your benefit in the middle game may hurt you in the endgame. And an acute sense of timing is essential. I've seen many examples of one player relaxing into a technical endgame only to find that his opponent is still in the creative middle game.

In the eleventh round of the 2002 Chess Olympiad in Slovenia, I had the black pieces against the top German player, Christopher Lutz. The game slowly simplified into a position without queens and only three pieces per player. Lutz brought his knights to the far side of the board where they became tangled up in seeking relatively insignificant gains. In an endgame this loss of time wouldn't be a major factor. But with his pieces on the other side of the board, I saw a chance to mount an attack on his king.

Even after it was clear what I was trying to do, Lutz underestimated the danger. He was already in endgame mode and wasn't able to switch back into a dynamic middle-game mentality to react to the threat. My small army soon cornered his king and forced him to resign. Misunderstanding the nature of the position and playing "in the wrong phase" as Lutz did can happen at other transition points as well.

Underestimating dynamic factors also happens in the early stages of play. Even a well-prepared player can delay thinking critically in the early middle game. Routine moves might pass in the opening, but they can lead to unpleasant surprises if your opponent is paying attention to more aggressive lines than you are. That is, if he is already playing the middle game while you're still in an opening mind-set.

These errors in transition occur in every area that involves planning and strategy. No matter what pursuit a smart planner is engaged in, he takes all three phases into account throughout. What sort of middle game is his opening going to lead to? Is it one he is prepared for? Does he have experience with this type of negotiation or battle or job or project? If so, how did the phases of the "game" evolve?

Austria's Rudolf Spielmann wrote we must "play the opening like a book, the middle game like a magician, and the endgame like a machine." Your goal should be not just to perform well in each phase but to make the transitions seamless.

We must now take the results of all this study and evaluation and transform it into action.

CHAPTER 10

THE ATTACKER'S ADVANTAGE

Even a bullet fears the brave.

—RUSSIAN SAYING

Flexing Your Intuition Leads to Strong Decision-Making

Intuition and instinct form the bedrock of our decision-making, especially the rapid-fire decisions that make up our daily lives. We don't have to analyze why we turn left here and right there on the way to work, we just do it. A chess player can spot a simple checkmate in three moves without hesitation even if he's never seen that exact position before in his life. We depend on these patterns the way we depend on our autonomic systems to keep us breathing. We are not like whales, which have to think about every breath.

You wouldn't want to consider every decision you make, and so you rely on patterns gleaned from experience. These are essential shortcuts and have no drawbacks as long as they are confined to the basic functions. Problems arise when we begin to rely on patterns for more sophisticated decisions in our lives. This stifles creativity and leads to a "one size fits all" approach to decision-making as we try to force the same patterns and solutions onto every problem we face.

With the sheer quantity of decisions we make every day, even small improvements and adaptations in our processes make a huge cumulative difference. It's like making a tiny enhancement in an assembly line that shaves a few precious seconds off the production of each car.

Big branches in the decision tree require extra caution. These are the forks in the road that leave us with no way back. It is an old chess maxim that "pawns can't move backward," which is more than a simple statement of the obvious. If I put my bishop on a bad square, I can later change my mind and move it back, and the same goes for any other piece. But pawns can only move in one direction, forward. We often talk about "committal moves," usually captures or other moves that change the position irrevocably. Every pawn move is of this sort and must therefore be considered more carefully.

Life's rules aren't as clear as those of chess; we can't always know when a decision will lead to irreversible consequences. As with detecting a crisis, sometimes it is obvious and at other times you have to go on instinct. It is always valuable to ask ourselves if we will be able to reverse course if our decision turns out poorly. What will our alternatives be if things go wrong? Is there a satisfactory alternative course where we can keep our options open longer?

This mentality requires us to overcome the desire to release the tension. Many bad decisions come from wanting to just get the process over to escape the pressure of having to make the decision. This is the worst type of haste, an unforced error. Resist it! If there is no benefit to making the decision at the moment and no penalty in delaying it, use that time to improve your evaluation, to gather more information, and to examine other options. As Margaret Thatcher put it, "I've learned one thing in politics. You don't make a decision until you have to."

As ever, my personal preference is to err on the side of intuition and optimism. Decisions derived from positive thinking may not be any more accurate than conservative decisions, but we definitely learn more from our mistakes. Over time our decisions will become more accurate as we exercise and hone our intuition. Most of us are happier when doing, when fulfilling the human need to push boundaries. As F. Scott Fitzgerald wrote, "Vitality shows not only in the ability to persist, but in the ability to start over." If we err and must begin again, we must. This vitality isn't only about quality of life; staying motivated and involved in decision-making is one key to improving it. One of the best ways to do this is to take the initiative, which puts positive pressure on you while challenging your competition. I like to say that the attacker always has the advantage.

The Aggression Double Standard

I received some unusual words of wisdom when at the age of seventeen I was awarded my first spot on the mighty Soviet Chess Olympiad team. We had traveled to Malta for a tournament with the Hungarians and were spending two days in Rome on the way back. My teammates were at least twice my age on average, so we had very different agendas on our free days. While the others took the opportunity to do some sightseeing, including a trip to the Vatican, I went to see *The Empire Strikes Back*, which I would never have been able to see in the USSR. I can't say what spiritual guidance my compatriots received at the Vatican, but there in the theater, I was being counseled by Yoda, as he warned Luke Skywalker that "anger, fear, aggression; the dark side of the Force are they." I was perplexed. In all honesty, at seventeen I completely sympathized with Luke's impatience with such a passive outlook. Didn't he have to go after Darth Vader and protect his friends? What was so bad about aggression?

As I got older and rose through the chess ranks, I realized that a persistent double standard was at work. In political and social life, the person who mounts a decisive attack is a bad guy, a black hat—except when he's not. We praise a CEO's management style as aggressive, but the average employee could be fired for being "aggressive." In some fields even ambition is viewed with suspicion. Anyone who obviously wants to get ahead can be criticized for trying to draw attention to himself. Even worse, they are accused of not being "a team player." At the same time, chess magazines celebrated my "aggressive chess" and my "violent attacks," in the same way that sports fans praise the aggressive attackers on their favorite teams. Such terms are provided special, almost always positive, meaning in the world of gaming and sport. We want "aggressive attackers" on our favorite teams even if we don't want them to move into our neighborhood. Or into the statehouse.

As I've mentioned, many people—old friends and perfect strangers alike—questioned my ability to move into politics. Citing my aggressive style of playing chess, they would ask, if attackers are born, not made, how could I change my stripes and succeed in an environment in which attacking is not only ineffective but can get you into real trouble? Of course I knew that I had the ability to adapt to a new environment. Anyone who really cares about something can do that. But in truth I think aggressiveness is as much of an asset in politics, business, and other walks of life as it is in chess. Putting limits on our ambition—and, yes, our aggressiveness—puts limits on our achievement. People who have an aggressive philosophy about their work also tend to be aggressive with their self-criticism. My concern is not about whether I'm being a nice guy; it's whether I'm constantly challenging myself, my environment, and those around me. It is the opposite of moral and physical complacency.

The Initiative Rarely Rings Twice

To be sure, the platitudes about winning being the "only thing" are as banal as the ones about winning not being important at all. What has always concerned me as a competitor is how to develop my own system of controlled aggression that would make me better at what I do—whether it's politics or chess. Aggression in this context means dynamism, innovation, improvement, courage, risk, and a willingness to take action. For me, the first essential lesson was learning how to unbalance the situation and take the initiative. You've got to bang a few rocks together to create fire.

When it's your move and you are creating the action instead of reacting to your opponent's actions, you control the flow of the game. In reacting, your opponent's moves become more limited and thus more predictable. From the lead position you can see farther ahead and continue to control the action. As long as you generate threats and pressure, you maintain the initiative. In chess this eventually leads to an attack that cannot be parried. In business it leads to greater market share. In negotiations it leads to a better deal. In politics it leads to a rise in the polls. In all such cases, when victory is imminent, the aggressor improves the quality of his material and also gains the luster of improved status—benefits that are both tangible and intangible. This is the attacker's advantage.

But it's not enough to simply attack. Once you've seized the initiative, you must exploit and feed it constantly, whether by mounting an all-or-nothing, lightning-quick attack or by taking the Boris Spassky approach of squeezing gradually. As Steinitz reminded us, the player with the advantage is obliged to attack or he will surely lose his advantage. A great attacker gets the greatest possible advantage out of a position without overstepping and trying to achieve more than what is possible. Be true to your own style, but only within the context of play as it exists on the chessboard.

A large part of using the initiative is mobility, flexibility, and diversion. The odds are against your winning a game against a strong player if you have only a single point of attack. Think of it in military terms:

stationing all the men in all the divisions of your army to attack one spot will leave you terribly exposed when you become the defender. This is what the Allies knew when they prepared for the famous D-day attack, Operation Overlord, which was the largest seaborne invasion in history. They developed numerous diversionary tactics—including a Potemkin-style dummy unit, complete with stage sets and fake equipment—to keep the Nazis too confused about their position and their intentions to prepare defenses.

Likewise, you should employ what chess players call the "principle of two weaknesses." Instead of becoming fixated on one spot, keep the pressure on—keep taking the initiative—so you can create multiple weak spots in your opponent's position. One weakness alone is rarely enough to cause defeat.

The opponent of an aggressive player is likely to become nervous and distracted from his game. No matter how secure his position appears to be, he will focus on the possibility of losing material, and on the likelihood of defeat. And this will inevitably lead him to changes in his approach and his thinking—changes that you, the aggressor, can exploit. This is the dynamic that Nimzowitsch had in mind when he wrote, "The threat is stronger than the execution." An attack doesn't even have to come to fruition to have a devastating effect on the enemy's position. If your opponent has to lose time rushing to defend one area, it may lead to an opportunity to win elsewhere. Prior to D-day, Allied double agents led the Nazis to believe the main attack was coming at Pas-de-Calais, which caused Hitler to send Rommel and his elite forces well away from the actual invasion site.

Nimzowitsch's famous phrase is also about perception, something akin to the old Wall Street line "Buy the rumor, sell the news." Anticipation of something's happening can be more powerful than the event itself or, put another way, is inseparable from the event itself.

An Attacker by Choice

As I look back on my career, I'm fascinated to see so many parallels between my development as a chess player and my development as a person. Although by any definition I played an aggressive, attacking game of chess throughout my career, my games became, over time, more solid and less speculative. In my thirties, after a decade as world champion, I was less likely to embark on an uncertain assault and more likely to be patient and wait for just the right moment to attack instead of rushing ahead. It's hard to know how much I was being affected by the general conservatism that often comes with age, but I think there was more at work here than that. Because I wasn't only playing differently—I was playing better. I was playing with real experience, and I had learned that defense followed by a well-timed counterattack against an overaggressive opponent could be more effective than always trying to meet fire with fire.

I no longer felt I had to prove something in every game by launching a blitzkrieg. I was taking a more professional approach: I was there to win, not make a statement. The people who are closest to me tell me that they see the same thing at work in the way I came to deal, later in life, with the media and in my business affairs. The two key events were the break with FIDE in 1993 and the collapse of the Professional Chess Association I started, which combined really took the wind from my sails, making me more circumspect. The FIDE break coincided with the painful dissolution of my first marriage and my separation from my wife and my daughter Polina.

Stability both on the board and in my private life returned in the second half of the 1990s. Owen Williams joined me as my full-time business agent, and I had started a new family that included an infant son, Vadim. In 1999, I launched an Internet company bearing my name, which literally turned me into a global brand. It also forced me to become aware of the broader, long-term effects that these family and business decisions would have. Suddenly it became clear to me that I could no longer pretend I was the rebel fighting the establishment; in many ways, I had become the establishment. And in truth I found it sometimes difficult to maintain the combative edge necessary to stay on top. In response, I spent some time reviewing my evolution as a chess player, looking back at old games and drilling down to understand how I had achieved my successes and, even more, how I could take the lessons of those successes—and, yes, failures—so I could remain true to the fundamentals in my new career in politics.

And what I now see is that despite these recent transformations, my best results both on and off the board always were and continue to be the product of an attacker's mind-set. The difference is that what came naturally to me at twenty-two often required more conscious decision-making at my current forty-three. Greater knowledge carries the burden of additional things to consider, and that opens the door for doubt to creep in. Overthinking numbs our instincts and turns what should be a quick decision into a mental committee meeting. The last thing I can now afford is to find myself sitting at the chessboard, or in a business meeting, wondering, "What would the young Garry Kasparov do?"

I used to attack because it was the only thing I knew. Now I attack because I know it works best. As a politician I know that there is always a time and place for diplomacy, but I also know that you win more often when you negotiate from a position of strength. And sometimes that means playing the aggressor.

> *What you can do or think you can do, begin it.*
> *For boldness has magic, power, and genius in it.*
> —GOETHE

The aggressive mentality involved in successful attacking requires a readiness to upset the status quo, even a passion for doing so. It means abandoning the more comfortable wait-and-see approach of the defensive position and pushing into the unknown.

Defending, by contrast, requires that we marshal our resources in a constant attempt to minimize our exposure to attack. Because he only has to ensure that his weaknesses are protected, the defender has fewer angles to cover. But as the pace of the world accelerates, the advantage is steadily moving toward the attacking side.

In the military realm, the art of defense is nearly obsolete today. The advent of heavy mobile armor ensured that World War I would be the last stagnant war of attrition. At the start of World War II, German tanks blitzkrieged across Europe, often taking more territory in a single day than the German army had captured in months twenty-five years earlier. Today we have laser-guided bombs that can destroy a cement bunker a hundred meters underground. Static defense is dead. Today's warfare is about hitting first and hitting hard.

We can see this trend mirrored across the rest of society. With things moving so quickly, a passive approach to investing and corporate strategy is as obsolete as siege fortresses and trench warfare. If you don't stay aggressively in front, you will quickly be left behind. Examples abound, but we see this particularly in the field of technology. Does the name AltaVista ring a bell? It was one of the many search engines that was pushed to the margins during the browser wars, first by Yahoo! and then by the Google juggernaut. By the time Google overtook it, Yahoo! had surged ahead of the curve enough to diversify its business into content areas such as news and entertainment and services such as free e-mail. AltaVista and other search engines such as Lycos and HotBot didn't and so were subsumed by their attackers.

By contrast, when Apple replaced the iPod mini, one of the most popular electronic products in history, with the nano, they were acknowledging that success in today's marketplace belongs to the attacker. Apple didn't wait around for its sales to slow or for another company to enter the market and take a bite out of its margins. They stepped right over their own product, released a new one, and even succeeded in persuading millions of users that the nano was better than the iPod they'd just bought. By contrast, as we saw earlier, Microsoft waited two years to begin work on a new Explorer browser, only making the effort when their market share had already started to fall significantly.

The Transition from Imitator to Innovator

The less visible but even more vital reason to invest in research and innovation is that you have to stay on the cutting edge if you are going to make a big impact. You can't suddenly switch from follower to leader because only the leader can see what's coming around the bend. Even the most successful imitators eventually become innovators if they want to expand their territory and become more successful. Those who fail to make this transition are usually supplanted by other imitators. As risky as innovation can be (one of my favorite sayings is "Pioneers get filled full of arrows"), failing to innovate is riskier still.

The transition from imitator to innovator is seen in every aspect of society. In chess, a young player can advance by imitating the top Grandmasters, but to challenge them he must produce his own ideas. Japanese goods were for many years reviled by Americans as cheap, poorly made knockoffs of U.S. and European products. The flood of inexpensive imports and imitations into the market rapidly created an enormous shift in the consumer electronics industry. Unable to adapt quickly enough, most American manufacturers soon abandoned the market or went out of business entirely. The Japanese were soon faced with the need to produce higher-end models with the new features consumers wanted. It didn't take long for imitators to give the Japanese companies a taste of their own medicine. Korea and Taiwan were quick to move into the lower-end market as the Japanese companies spent more money on research and development. The Japanese became innovators. Just like Darwinism in nature, innovation is quite literally about survival. We have to keep evolving, and that means staying aggressive instead of standing still.

The Will to Attack

As Tartakower said, "The first essential for an attack is the will to attack." All of our planning and evaluation skills are academic if they aren't combined with the nerve to employ them and to strike when the opportunity arises. If you're already in a fight, you want the first blow to be the last and you had better be the one to throw it.

Attacking requires perfect timing as well as nerve. Knowing the right time to attack is as much an art as a science, and even for the best it's often guesswork. The window of opportunity is usually small. No neon sign appears to announce that a big opportunity is right around the corner. Most of all, detecting opportunities requires letting go of assumptions of all kinds. This is especially true in quiet positions, those periods of stability that seem unlikely to produce attacking chances. We are often reminded never to underestimate our opponents, but overestimating them also leads to missed opportunities. If you keep an open mind and consider an aggressive option first in every situation, you won't miss those chances. Assume it is the right time to strike!

Pushing the action gives us more options and a greater ability to control our fate, which creates positive energy and confidence. This energy we create is no small thing. Tal once said that perhaps the worst move of his life was one he didn't make, a speculative sacrifice he pondered for forty minutes before uncharacteristically declining. Attackers may sometimes regret bad moves, but it is much worse to forever regret an opportunity you allowed to pass you by.

part three

CHAPTER 11

QUESTION SUCCESS

Success Is the Enemy of Future Success

On November 9, 1985, I achieved the great goal of my young life: I became the world champion of chess. During the celebration afterward I was taken aside by Rona Petrosian, the wife of the former world champion. "I feel sorry for you," she said. "The greatest day of your life is over." What a thing to say at a victory party!

But those words resonated in my head in the many years that followed, and now, after a lifetime as a competitor, I know firsthand that one of the most dangerous enemies you can face is complacency. I've seen—both in myself and my competitors—how satisfaction can lead to a lack of vigilance, then to mistakes and missed opportunities. Success and satisfaction may be our goals, but they can also lead to bad habits that will impede greater success and satisfaction.

The Gravity of Past Success

After that huge early victory I spent the next fifteen years in a constant battle to augment my strengths and eliminate my weaknesses. I became convinced that if I worked unrelentingly and diligently and played to the best of my ability, no one could defeat me. And I believed that until the day I retired in March 2005. How, then, can I explain my loss to my countryman Kramnik in our 2000 world championship match? In chapter 2 we looked at his success purely at the chess level, by analyzing how he succeeded in selecting and controlling the battlefield for our contest. The strategic failure on my part had deeper origins, however.

In great part my own success had made it difficult, if not impossible, for me to see what was going on in the championship tournament against Kramnik. In the two years prior to the October 2000 match, I had been playing some of the best chess of my life, refuting the critics who had predicted the end of my reign at the top. They kept citing my advanced age; at thirty-five I was already a decade older than most of my opponents. But I kept winning. In 1999 I pushed my record rating to new heights and was in the middle of a "grand slam" tournament winning streak when I started preparations for the world championship match. I felt as though I could move mountains at the chessboard. So how did Kramnik's infuriating Berlin Defense stop me in my tracks?

Ironically, my years of success had made me vulnerable. One of the strongest points of my game had always been my ability to adapt and meet new challenges, and Kramnik used that strategy against me. Despite my discomfort in the positions he led me into, I kept insisting to myself that I could adjust as the match played out and that I had enough time to recover and win. In my first world championship match, with Karpov in 1984–85, there had been no limit to the number of games we would play, and I was able to adapt, alter my strategy, and recover the lead. But in a match of just sixteen games there just wasn't enough time.

I had been outprepared by my young opponent, and I was so stunned that I was incapable of even acknowledging that I was in serious trouble. When the realization finally hit me, it was already late in the short match and I went from feeling sure I would recover to believing it was impossible. I put up a little fight toward the end, but it wasn't enough. I ended the fifteen-game match with two losses and not a single win.

I lost because I was overconfident and complacent. Even while it was happening, it was difficult for me to credit my onetime student with possessing the talent to outfox me. Nor did it ever occur to me that Kramnik could—or would—prepare better than I had. I had also neglected to consider that he had been one of my assistants in my 1995 world championship match against Anand. He knew all my habits and all my tactics. Instead of devising a strategy to use that knowledge against him, I ignored it. And flush with past success, I couldn't conceive there were any serious weaknesses in my game.

This is what I call the gravity of past success. Winning creates the illusion that everything is fine. We think only of the positive result without considering all the things that went wrong—or that could have gone wrong—along the way. After a victory we want to celebrate, not analyze. We replay the triumphant moment in our mind until it looks as though it were inevitable.

Most of us are guilty of the same bad habit in our day-to-day lives. My advice? The old saying "If it ain't broke, don't fix it" should be left to the plumbing trade and never applied to how we lead our lives at home and at work. Question the status quo at all times, *especially* when things are going well. When something goes wrong, you naturally want to do it better the next time, but you must train yourself to want to do it better *even when things go right*. Failing to do this leads to stagnation and eventual breakdown. For me, it led to a crushing defeat.

Competition and Anticomplacency Tactics

Failure due to complacency exists in every enterprise. In competitive environments such as the military and the corporate world, it almost always springs from doing "business as usual" while the competition is catching up and surpassing us. The consequences of resting on reputation and outdated experience can be dire.

In 1919, during the Russian civil war, Marshal Kliment Voroshilov—a favorite of Stalin's—routed the White Guard with a swarm of massed cavalry units. In the years before mechanized warfare, it worked brilliantly. But when the Germans invaded in 1941, the Red Army veterans leading the Soviet troops foolishly still believed that horses were paramount. When the Nazi armored divisions rolled in, the mounted Red Army was completely ineffectual, and Hitler's tanks encircled Leningrad.

Horses were no match for tanks and artillery. American car companies in the seventies were no match for new Japanese production and management techniques. Constant reinvention is a necessity in fast-moving areas such as manufacturing and technology.

So how do we inspire ourselves to keep pushing for better results? Competition is one inspiring way. After all, who runs a race wanting to come in second? Who grows up wanting to be the vice president? Who sits down at a chessboard ready to relinquish his king? Athletes often talk about finding motivation in the desire to meet their own challenges and play their own best game, without worrying about their opponents. Though there is some truth to this, I find it a little disingenuous. While everyone has a unique way to get motivated and stay that way, all athletes thrive on competition, and that means beating someone else, not just setting a personal best. Ask the Olympic runner who breaks his personal record, or even the world record, and finishes a close second how good he feels. We don't need to wonder if he would trade a tenth of a second for a gold medal instead of silver.

We all work harder, run faster, when we know someone is right on our heels. Some of my best performances came in the heat of close competition. Just as racing dogs go much faster after a "rabbit," we push ourselves to greater exertions if we have a competitor matching us stride for stride to the finish line.

There can be no finer example of the inspiring powers of competition to shatter the status quo than Hungary's Judit Polgar. Polgar, the only woman among the top several hundred players on the international rating list, gained fame for her sparkling attacking chess. If, based on Polgar's games, to "play like a girl" meant anything in chess, it would mean relentless aggression. Polgar first came on the international scene at the age of ten, and at twelve was winning open international tournaments. In 1991 she broke Bobby Fischer's thirty-year-old record to become the youngest Grandmaster ever at the age of fifteen. (That record has since become a popular target and, thanks to the proliferation of the once rare GM title, has been broken many times. It is now held by Ukraine's Sergey Karjakin, who in 2002 became a GM at twelve years, seven months.)

Along with her two chess-playing older sisters, Susan and Sofia, Polgar was homeschooled by her father, Lazlo, who had a theory that "geniuses can be created." The experimental curriculum he devised for the girls focused on chess, and it's hard to argue with the results. The issue of nature versus nurture has always been a hot topic in chess. I suppose that since the Polgars are sisters they don't resolve the debate either way, but their upbringing and development certainly make a good case for nurture.

Enclaves where women's chess was traditional had produced some strong players, but for most of the game's history the few women who played chess competently were regarded as curiosities. The former Soviet republic of Georgia boasted Nona Gaprindashvili and Maia Chiburdanidze, two of the first women to make inroads into the international chess world in the sixties and seventies. Like most women players they limited their growth by concentrating on women-only events, especially in the critical early years of their development. Over time, everyone had simply accepted that that was the way it was.

The Polgars changed all that. With a few exceptions for official events such as the women's Chess Olympiad—where the sisters twice composed the first three boards of the winning Hungarian team—they shunned women-only events and sought out the toughest competition. Susan, the eldest, was pushed out into the rough-and-tumble world of international tournament chess as a teenager and became one of the first women to receive the "men's" Grandmaster title. At the age of fourteen, in Rome, middle sister Sofia scored one of the astonishing open tournament results on record, battering a field of Grandmasters. And after winning the Hungarian national championship in 1991 at the age of fifteen, Judit said she would only consider playing on the "men's" Chess Olympiad team. What could the Hungarian federation say? Thanks to the Polgars the adjective *men's* before events and the "affirmative action" women's titles such as *Woman Grandmaster* have become anachronisms (though they are still in use).

By seeking out and often besting the toughest competition, the Polgars showed that there are no inherent limitations to their aptitude—an idea that many male players refused to accept until they had unceremoniously been crushed by a twelve-year-old with a ponytail. In 2005, Judit returned to chess after taking a year off to have a child. Her first engagement after her return was a tough one, the Corus supertournament in the Netherlands, and she finished with a positive score and gained rating points. On the October 2005 rating list, Judit Polgar, at twenty-nine, was ranked number eight in the world, just four points behind Vladimir Kramnik.

It may well be that the Polgars were partly pushed to excellence by their desire to prove that women can be as capable at the board as men. What's most notable for our purposes is that they became better players than any other women by facing tougher competition than those women.

I too would have been unable to reach my potential without a nemesis like Karpov breathing down my neck and pushing me every step of the way. When a new generation of chess players emerged in the nineties and Karpov ceased to be the main threat to my dominant position, I had to refocus and find new sources of inspiration. So I dedicated myself to fighting back against the new wave of talented young stars, something few world champions had managed to do for long.

Without Karpov to focus my energies on, I became more heavily involved with chess politics and sponsorship activities. This period also marked my increased involvement in computer chess and other exhibitions. Not until 1998, after my loss to IBM's computer Deep Blue, did I realize I had become distracted from chess. I rededicated myself to working harder than ever on my game—and on beating human opponents. The results were evident, and despite my match loss to Kramnik in 2000 I played some of the best chess of my life in the years 1999–2001.

Every good player has his or her own methods. After a fifty-year career, the amazing Viktor Korchnoi has kept his competitive fires burning and is still playing high-level chess well into his seventies. "Viktor the Terrible" has led a difficult and colorful life both on and off the board, defecting from the USSR in 1976 after years of battles with the Soviet authorities. He became even more of a thorn in their side after he fled to the West, first to the Netherlands and then to his current home in Switzerland. It became difficult for the Soviet censors to keep the defector's name out of the news when he was winning so many tournaments and defeating the top Soviet players. Three times he faced the much younger Karpov in world championship contests, failing each time but comforting himself with his bittersweet title: Strongest Player Never to Become World Champion. Korchnoi has had a revenge of sorts by continuing to play competitive chess while Karpov—twenty years younger—has largely retired from the rigors of tournament play. When he was the age at which I retired, Korchnoi was not yet at his peak!

Despite his impressive career Korchnoi has always been able to play as if he has something more to prove. Defying age is not nearly enough for him; he is not content just to turn up and move the pieces around. Korchnoi enjoys showing players a half century his junior that they still have something to learn from him. At a tournament in 2004, Korchnoi defeated the Norwegian prodigy Grandmaster Magnus Carlsen, a triumph of a seventy-three-year-old over a fourteen-year-old.

Korchnoi has maintained his drive by refusing to look back at what would be the glory days for just about anyone else. He is still driven by the game of chess and by an earnest desire to beat his opponent, not merely to do his best. Korchnoi is an inspiration to me because I also believe it's essential to have benchmarks in our lives to keep us alert. In chess and other sports we have ratings, opponents, and tournaments, so things seem clear, but as I've left the professional world of chess, I see that more is required.

Regardless of the methods we use to motivate ourselves, we have to create our own goals and standards and then keep raising them. It can feel a bit paradoxical to muster up the confidence that we are the best but still compete as if we were outsiders and underdogs. But that's what it takes. It is just as hard to change a working formula, but anyone who wants to excel over a long career will find it necessary to do both things: nurture your inherent strengths but be nimble enough to develop new avenues of attack. Despite having won eight gold medals over three Olympics, Carl Lewis still wanted more at the age of thirty-five. To qualify for the 1996 Olympic Games in Atlanta, he embarked on an entirely new training program, leaving behind everything that had worked for him. He knew that his age and injuries created new challenges. He went on to win another gold in Atlanta, and he did it by not being afraid to change what worked.

Finding ways to maintain our concentration and motivation is the key to fighting complacency. Maybe you don't have a rating system at work or at home the way professional chess or tennis players do, but that doesn't mean you can't develop one. What metrics can you contrive to measure your performance? Certainly money can be valued and easily measured, but it can't be the only thing. Perhaps you should create your own "happiness index," which can be as simple as a mental or actual list of things that motivate you and give you pleasure and satisfaction.

Before you can fight, you have to know what you are fighting for. Every parent says he or she wants to spend more time with his or her kids, but how many people actually know, down to the hour, how much time they do spend together each week, each month? How many hours at work do you waste playing solitaire or surfing the Web? What if you kept track and knew the answer? Then you would have a target to pursue. Most of us need to develop a more helpful technique than the vague promise of the cliché "Just do it." Anticipating Nike's ad agency by two centuries, Goethe wrote, "Knowing is not enough; we must apply. Willing is not enough; we must do."

In Favor of Contradiction

The motivation to question our methods can come from within, or it may come from without. In the business world, only an unusual boss will hire employees who approach things differently and who will challenge his ideas and practices. It takes great willpower and self-confidence to surround ourselves with smart, talented people who we know will confront us. No one enjoys being contradicted or "corrected"—there's a constant risk of losing authority or creating an anarchy of mixed messages.

But the leader who is willing to risk these things has the potential for extraordinary success.

These people are extraordinary because they have overcome the dread of being challenged, which is the same as the childish fear of simply being wrong. This fear can be crippling to your development and success. I've learned from my years of playing competitive chess to trust in my ability to use the opposition to make myself stronger and to gather more information about the process at hand. Whenever you feel threatened, remember the words of Emerson, who wrote, "Let me never fall into the vulgar mistake of dreaming that I am persecuted whenever I am contradicted."

Feudal and caste systems have just about died out in most nations across the globe, but they are alive and well in the chess world. National and international federations establish classes and categories based on a complex rating system that allows players to compete for prizes against opponents who are at a similar level. First-category players aren't allowed to participate in the second-category competition any more than a twenty-year-old could play in the under-twelve championship. Of course there are no restrictions in the opposite direction. An ambitious novice is free to get killed in the "open" section where the highest-rated players compete. So no one could complain that it was unfair when I won the Soviet national under-eighteen tournament at the age of twelve.

If it is challenges that help us improve, why then—apart from prize money—doesn't everyone want to play in the open section of a tournament? There's no doubt about it: you'll learn more from nine losses to strong opponents than from six wins and three losses against players who are at roughly your own level. The same thing holds true with players who don't attend tournaments but play against chess software. A PC program at its maximum strength will wipe out any casual player without mercy. Ironically, the main task of chess software companies today is to find ways to make the program weaker, not stronger, and to provide enough options that any user can pick from different levels and the machine will try to make enough mistakes to give him a chance. So how much of a chance should you ask for against the mighty machine?

Every person has to find the right balance between confidence and correction, but my rule of thumb is, lose as often as you can take it. Playing in the open section and going 0-9 every time is going to crush your spirit long before you get good enough to make a decent score. Unless you have a superhuman ego, or totally lack one, a constant stream of negativity will leave you too depressed and antagonized to make the necessary changes.

But as much as you enjoy winning, remember that winning every time is not ideal. Setbacks and losses are both inevitable and essential if you're going to improve and become a good, even great, competitor. The art is in avoiding catastrophic losses in the key battles. This same principle also applies in the real world, where, if you're well insulated by your supporters and staff, you can believe that you are right virtually all of the time. It's not only dictators and pharaohs who are always right. Politicians and CEOs tend to both attract and hire like-minded staffers and employees. They gain energy by talking with their avid supporters and accuse critics of not being supportive. When things go wrong, they assign the blame to others. It is dangerously easy to go from succeeding in business or politics because you are often correct to surrounding yourself with others who tell you you are correct because of who you are.

The Difference Between Better and Different

If you can learn to accept criticism and invite your people to present new information—particularly that which may contradict an idea or practice that you hold dear—you will quickly learn to adopt new and potentially powerful methods into your game plan. Learn to see value in other methods and take what you need from them to improve—but not necessarily replace—your own.

CHAPTER 12

THE INNER GAME

The Game Can Be Won Before You Get to the Board

South American liberator Simón Bolívar said, "Only an inexperienced soldier believes that all is lost after being defeated for the first time." In the weeks and months after my nemesis Vladimir Kramnik took the world championship title from me, in November 2000 in London, I had plenty of time to absorb exactly what Kramnik had achieved and how he had done it. I spent hours identifying and analyzing the weaknesses of mine that he had exploited, and hours more figuring out how to turn the tables on Kramnik and exploit his flaws. We played over a dozen games after that match, all of them draws but one. The lone victory was mine. That win came in the final round of a supertournament, and I had to win that game if I was to overtake Kramnik for first place. Ironically his opening was the very same Berlin Defense that had so frustrated me in the all-important London match. That, along with the substantial lead I had managed to maintain in the rankings, gave me a small bit of consolation. All that time I had spent finding the holes in my game paid off with a satisfying victory against Kramnik, but even more important, it was an essential part of my psychological recuperation after the loss of my world championship title. Getting back into the ring after a bruising loss is never easy, especially when you know that your opponent has been emboldened by your perceived weakness. That's why I always think of Simón Bolívar and remember that the experienced soldier who studies the battlefields in the aftermath of the war returns with both wisdom and renewed courage.

Few things are as psychologically brutal as serious chess. You spend five or six hours in total concentration, at war with another mind. In the background is a ticking clock. There is nowhere to hide, and you have no teammates to toss the ball to, no referees to blame, no dice to roll or new cards to turn over. Chess is often called a one hundred percent information game, because both players know everything that is going on all the time. When you lose, it's because the other player beat you, plain and simple. In this, chess has much more in common with boxing than other sports or games. As my 1993 world championship challenger Nigel Short once said in an interview, "Chess is ruthless: you've got to be prepared to kill people."

You can't overestimate the importance of psychology in chess, and as much as some players try to downplay it, I believe that winning requires a constant and strong psychology not just at the board but in every aspect of your life.

The Storm Before the Calm

It begins with intense preparation, which requires that you motivate yourself to work long, grueling, lonely hours. It often feels like a Sisyphean task, since you know that perhaps only ten percent of your analysis will ever see the light of day. And then the game is imminent, the adrenaline is flowing, and you're in a battle to control your nerves and fears. Some players lose sleep or appetite, some do last-minute preparation and focus on the game, while others watch a movie or take a walk to clear their head. I always knew something was wrong if I wasn't on edge before a game. Nervous energy is the ammunition we take into any mental battle. If you don't have enough of it, your concentration will fade. If you have a surplus, the results can be explosive.

Several times in my career I had an extraordinary feeling before a game that no matter who my opponent was or what he did, I was going to tear him limb from limb. This happened in 1993 before my game with Karpov in the Linares, Spain, supertournament. Even though I was playing with the slight disadvantage of the black pieces, I was bouncing off the walls in anticipation. I had a strange feeling that something phenomenal was going to happen.

My old rival Karpov and I were tied for first place with only four rounds to play. My trainer Sergey Makarichev, sensing how optimistic I was, boasted before the game that I was going to wipe Karpov out this time. Indeed that was what happened, although no one could have predicted the comedic twist at the conclusion. After sacrificing a pawn and seizing the initiative, I reached a dominating position. My pieces quickly pushed Karpov's back against the first rank, which was highly unusual. On move twenty-four I promoted a pawn, announcing, "Queen," and looking over to the referee with the implied request that he deliver me a second queen. But before I received the referee's response, Karpov played an illegal move! He claimed that since I hadn't yet actually placed a new queen on the board, he could choose which piece my pawn would be promoted to, and that he chose a bishop, a much weaker piece. The little farce was quickly resolved. I got my new queen and Karpov resigned three moves later. That win was part of a five-game stretch I consider one of the best series of tournament rounds of my life: four wins and a draw against the world's top players to clinch the tournament victory. In hindsight I know that much of the credit for that win goes to the dynamic of psychology. I went into the tournament with a premonition of victory, and there is much more to that than simply the power of positive thinking. Creative and competitive energy is a tangible thing, and if we can feel it, so can our opponents.

Don't Get Distracted While Trying to Distract

Like just about everyone on earth, real chess players fall between the literary caricatures of the ultrarational James Bond villain Kronsteen and Vladimir Nabokov's psychotic Luzhin. In my experience most of them are bunched toward the rational end of the bell curve, but there are notable exceptions. The incredible story of Viktor Korchnoi's 1978 world championship match against Anatoly Karpov in the Philippines is enough to make anyone wonder if chess players might indeed be crazy.

Tensions between the two sides were at a peak before the match even began. The "hated defector" Korchnoi was challenging the full might of the Soviet machine and its champion Karpov. Countless petty protests were filed by both sides before they started the first game. They argued about the flags on the table, the height and style of the chairs, the color of the yogurt Karpov ate during the games. But none of these were as bizarre as the story of Dr. Vladimir Zukhar, a psychology professor who came to Baguio City as part of Karpov's entourage.

Zukhar sat in the audience and stared directly at Korchnoi during every game of the world championship. His association with Karpov and his disconcerting mien led the superstitious Korchnoi and his overprotective team to suspect foul play of a supernatural kind. Zukhar was accused of being a parapsychologist who was attempting to disrupt Korchnoi's thinking. Korchnoi's team asked that Zukhar not be allowed to sit too close to the stage, while the Soviets fought every request and responded with their own demands. Thus began a bizarre escapade that saw Zukhar changing seats daily, often flanked by members of Korchnoi's delegation. Prior to game seventeen of the match, Korchnoi even refused to play unless Zukhar moved farther back, a protest that cost the challenger eleven minutes on his clock, time he could later have used when he found himself in severe time trouble. Later, Korchnoi brought in his own "parapsychologist, neurologist, and hypnotist" to combat Zukhar's powers.

The saga continued in similar fashion throughout the match. Was it all posturing? Or is it really possible that the two greatest chess players on the planet, and their closest associates, were distracted by such sideshows during the most important match of their careers? Karpov won the final game—with Zukhar sitting up front—to win the thirty-two-game match by a single point. I often wonder how much better Korchnoi would have done if he hadn't invested so much energy responding to Karpov's provocations and speculating about whether Karpov was receiving secret messages in his yogurt. Incidentally, Karpov's first victory came in game eight, after he startled his opponent—and the fans—by refusing to shake Korchnoi's hand before the game. Another psychological gambit well played?

Breaking the Spell of Pressure

Years of competition got me used to the tension that came with each game and important event. It wasn't so easy for me at the start of my career, however. In January 1978, at the age of fourteen—an aging prodigy—I participated in the Sokolsky Memorial tournament in Minsk with the hopes of earning a score good enough to qualify for my master title. I also needed to follow up my junior successes. After clinching two consecutive national junior titles I had failed to win the world under-sixteen championship in 1976 and 1977. Meanwhile, my closest junior rival, Artur Jussupow, had just won the world under-twenty title. Making matters worse, I would be a conspicuous outsider at the tournament. It was highly unusual for a junior to be invited to play in a strong event in another Soviet republic—from Azerbaijan to Byelorussia in this case. I was allowed to play only at the insistence of my mentor Botvinnik, so success was critical for both our reputations. And to cap it all off, I was a bit scared of some of my experienced opponents.

My mother came up with an idea. "Garik," she told me the day before the first round, "you can do well here, but before each game I want you to memorize some lines from Pushkin's poem *Eugene Onegin*. It will sharpen your senses." I followed her advice, and *Onegin* became the magic feather that distracted me from my anxiety. I won my first games and my confidence returned. In the end, I not only scored enough points to qualify for my master title but I also won the tournament—with a little help from our national poet. I can still recall the opening lines, albeit in Russian of course.

> *My uncle—high ideals inspire him;*
> *but when past joking he fell sick,*
> *he really forced one to admire him—*
> *and never played a shrewder trick.*
> *Let others learn from his example!*

Feeling uneasy under pressure is completely natural; when we begin to feel nonchalant about new challenges, it may be time to worry. If everything seems easy, you aren't pushing yourself hard enough. If you don't keep up your psychological strength, you won't be able to respond well when faced with setbacks. Psychological muscles atrophy from disuse just as physical and mental ones do. If it has been a while since you experienced the nervous thrill of trying something new, perhaps you've been avoiding a challenge for too long. We all need a regular diet of change as well as a healthy nervous energy to maintain our defenses.

We must have those defenses in good working order when failure strikes. It is difficult to learn from a tough loss and still come out the next day believing we are the best. It takes a strong mind to balance these somewhat contradictory story lines, especially after a particularly crushing defeat. Our theory of mind over matter can also work against us if we are convinced things are hopeless. One defeat quickly leads to another, then another. This can happen over a single tournament or even a career, falling into a rut of failure.

Staying Objective When the Chips Are Down

In my 1986 championship match with Karpov in Leningrad, I was well in the lead when I suddenly crashed with three losses in a row, leaving the match tied with five games remaining. After the third loss, in game nineteen, I had an emergency session with my coaches about what to do with white in the next game. Should I force a quick draw to stabilize myself and recover, or should I fight on as usual? "Why not fight?" I said. "I've just lost three, how could I possibly lose four in a row?" Grandmaster Mikhail Gurevich, who has plenty of experience in both chess and casinos, reminded me that playing the odds that way doesn't work. When you play roulette, you can lose many times in a row by betting on black every time. It's sad but true, and it's a lesson worth attending to in every enterprise in life: it makes no sense to believe that faring poorly now means you'll do better later. There are no cosmic scales that will eventually balance out on their own. I took his advice and made a short draw in game twenty, drew game twenty-one, and then, fully recovered, scored a crushing victory in game twenty-two to retake the lead and hold on to my title.

Casinos often put up digital signs next to roulette wheels that display the last dozen winning numbers, encouraging people to believe that they can gain an advantage with this information when in reality it is worthless. The wheel doesn't know how the last spin came out. It is dangerous to fool ourselves into believing that something is due to happen when there is no relation between the events of the past and what could occur in the present. To believe the casino is to do little more than to follow superstition.

Pretenders to the Crown and Fatal Flaws

Along with the eternal "Who was the greatest ever?" debate, one of the most popular discussions at chess clubs or on the Internet message boards is who deserves the dubious title of "greatest player never to be world champion." Throughout chess history we encounter great players who came close but never ascended to chess Olympus. These legends were not lacking in chess skills, and indeed they created many of the game's enduring masterpieces. But for one reason or another, they were never awarded the ultimate honor.

When we ask why these great players never quite made it to the top, we have to go beyond shrugging our shoulders and blaming it on fate. It's not always clear precisely where to place the blame, and each case is different and offers insight into the psychology of failure.

Supporters of the dynamic Russian player Mikhail Chigorin can't say he didn't have his chances. Twice he jousted for the world championship against Wilhelm Steinitz, toward the end of the nineteenth century, and both times he lost. Throughout his career Chigorin fought against the conventional wisdom, sometimes to a fault. He was never able to fully harness his wild creativity. Once he fixated on an idea, his theoretical point became more important to him than winning, and this lack of competitive pragmatism prevented him from making it to the top.

Chigorin teaches us that we cannot sacrifice results to a blind belief in our methods, no matter how innovative they may be. I see in him a tendency, which many have, to respond to a setback by telling himself that he didn't follow through enough, that if only he had gone even further in the same direction, things would have turned out better. The lesson here is that you must rely on your inner observer to look at your results dispassionately, and to push your ego aside long enough to fully and rigorously question your approach. Had Chigorin been able to rein in his fantasy on just a few occasions, the world might have had its first Russian champion decades before Alekhine.

If any chess player can be forgiven for cursing the Fates it would be Akiba Rubinstein. Now, nearly a century after he joined the elite, the quality of his chess is still above reproach. But a certain sporting impracticality cost him dearly on more than one occasion. Rubinstein was unwilling or unable to consider both the larger tournament situation as well as the game at hand, and he lost sight of the big picture and took unnecessary risks. If he only needed a draw to finish first, his nature would still push him to play a complicated winning attempt that might end in disaster. But his more consequential failings were away from the board. A championship contender in the early twentieth century needed charisma and a knack for cultivating sponsorship, and Rubinstein was the epitome of the shy and unsocial chess player. No matter how great his chess skills, he lacked the people skills to be a self-promoter and fund-raiser.

So despite his many tournament successes Rubinstein never succeeded in putting together the money that was needed to challenge Lasker. The timid Pole just wasn't capable of the kind of posturing and heated public exchanges that guaranteed a place at the table. The bold Cuban Capablanca soon surpassed him as the number one contender. It's true that in chess as in politics, fund-raising and glad-handing matter. Only in an ideal world does the most qualified candidate win the election. In the real world, the moment you believe you are entitled to something is exactly when you are ripe to lose it to someone who is fighting harder.

Rubinstein wasn't the only leading player to retire without getting a shot at the world championship. Paul Keres spent decades in the highest ranks of chess before and after the Second World War. The Estonian-born Soviet's opportunity to challenge for the title was hindered by the outbreak of war, but after the war ended, Keres lost out again because the Soviet authorities preferred the "good Russian" Botvinnik, and they allowed him to advance. Fate aside, however, Keres had multiple chances to qualify for the world championship and always came up short. I cannot assign any particular failing to his chess, but because of his track record I am skeptical that he would have been a match for Botvinnik under the bright lights of the world championship stage.

David Bronstein did earn a shot at Botvinnik. Their 1951 match ended in a draw, and because chess traditionally entitles the incumbent to "draw odds"—i.e., the champion keeps the crown if the match is drawn—Botvinnik retained his title. Ever after, Bronstein liked to tell his students that if he hadn't lost the penultimate game of that match, they would listen to him "as if to the oracle of Delphi!"

The young Bronstein arrived at his match against the living legend Botvinnik having already achieved, for him, a great victory just by reaching the championship match. Bronstein was the most creative player of his generation, and he seemed to have all the ingredients necessary to bring down the world champion. But having set his sights on reaching the final, he found it impossible to raise them to winning the match itself. Taking pride in our achievements mustn't distract us from our ultimate goals. A marathoner who makes good time over twenty-six miles isn't going to get credit unless he finishes the last 385 yards. After reaching the heights, Bronstein was unable to maintain his concentration and play his best chess. He committed several of the worst errors of his career during his match with Botvinnik.

A defeat can be doubly damaging when we feel we've done our best and still failed. This is contrary to every parent's words of consolation to a child whose soccer team has lost: "You did your best." We are supposed to feel better knowing that even if the outcome wasn't positive, we couldn't have done any more. And yet, someone with aspirations to be the champion of the world does not want to hear that he did his best and was still convincingly beaten. Indeed, could there be anything worse?

Thomas Szasz, the famous "antipsychiatrist," wrote, "There is no psychology; there is only biography and autobiography." I think of that statement and I'm reminded, as a chess player, that results are what matter in the end. We don't live our lives with motivational tricks and ploys; we cannot fool ourselves for long. Perhaps those who fail under pressure are those who believe too much in their methods of motivation and allow them to become a distraction. Overthinking can distract us from our concrete objectives.

It comes down to making the best moves and reaching the correct decisions. To do this we must accept responsibility for our results. Every decision we make builds our character and forms the basis of our future decisions. We must not be relegated to a supporting role in our own lives. The inner game *is* the game. It's not psychology. It is life as it should be lived, an autobiography in progress.

CHAPTER 13

MAN VS. MACHINE

Enter the Machines

One entity in the world is completely free of gender prejudice and preconceived ideas about who is stronger, men or women, and that is the computer. Throughout the history of mechanical and digital computing, chess has been near the forefront of designers' minds. As soon as man invents a machine, it seems the next step is to turn his creation into a chess player. One reason is that so many geniuses and inventors have played the game—maybe not brilliantly, but with passion and interest. Chess has always maintained a position as, in Goethe's words, "a touchstone of the intellect." Just about everyone who created a "thinking machine" was quick to put it to the test of mastering the world's most respected game.

The first chess-playing "machine," known as the Turk, was introduced to the general public in 1769. The Hungarian engineer Baron Wolfgang von Kempelen created it for the amusement of the Hapsburg empress Maria Theresa. This purely mechanical device was hidden beneath a majestic mannequin dressed as a Turk. Predictably, it was a fake: its outstanding playing strength was in fact supplied by a chess master cleverly secreted inside the device.

The main challenge of chess programming is the large number of continuations involved. In an average position there are about forty legal moves. So if you consider every reply to each move, you have sixteen hundred positions. After two moves there are 2.5 million positions, after three moves, 4.1 billion. The average game lasts forty moves, so the numbers involved are beyond astronomical.

Remarkably, the first computer program was written before a computer existed that could run it. Its creator was Alan Turing, the British mathematician who led the group that broke the German Enigma code during World War II and is widely considered the father of modern computer science. He developed a series of instructions for automated chess play, but since there was as yet no machine that could execute this first-ever chess code, Turing worked through it himself, on paper. Around the same time, in the United States, another great mathematical mind, Claude Shannon, was outlining several strategies computers could use to play chess.

In 1950 the nuclear laboratory of Los Alamos was the unlikely site of the next step forward in chess computing. When the gigantic machine MANIAC I was delivered, the scientists tested it by writing a chess program. After playing against itself and then losing to a strong player—despite being given an extra queen—the machine beat a young woman who had just learned the game. It was the first time a human had lost to a computer in a game of intellectual skill.

The next advances came in the form of smarter programming, in which the developers "taught" the computer how to avoid wasting time considering inferior moves. The mathematical "alpha-beta" chess algorithm was developed, which allowed the program to rapidly prune out weak moves and see further ahead. This is a brute-force method, now in universal use, in which the program stops evaluating any move that returns an evaluation score inferior to the score of the current first-move choice. The first programs that used this method, running on some of the fastest computers of the day, reached a respectable playing strength. By the 1970s, early personal computers could defeat most amateurs.

The next leap came from the famous Bell Laboratories. Ken Thompson, creator of the UNIX operating system, built a special-purpose chess machine with hundreds of chips. His machine, which he named Belle, was able to search about 180,000 positions per second. Supercomputers at the time could only manage 5,000. Seeing up to nine moves ahead during a game, Belle could play at the level of a human master and far better than any other chess machine. It won just about every computer chess event from 1980 to 1983, before it was finally surpassed by giant Cray supercomputers.

As the technology developed, new consumer chess programs with names such as Sargon, Chessmaster, and Fritz benefited, in particular from the faster processors engineered by Intel. Dedicated machines made a comeback thanks to a generation of chess machines designed at Carnegie Mellon University. Professor Hans Berliner was a computer scientist as well as a world champion at correspondence chess, an ancient form of playing the game through the mail. His machine, HiTech, was later surpassed by the creations of his graduate students Murray Campbell and Feng-hsuing Hsu. They took their computer champion, Deep Thought, and joined IBM, where their project was rechristened Deep Blue.

The Deep Blue machine that I faced in matches in 1996 and 1997—more on them in a moment—consisted of an IBM SP2 server equipped with a large number of special chess chips. This combination was capable of searching 200 million positions per second. Like all modern chess machines, Deep Blue also had access to a vast database of preprogrammed opening positions culled from human Grandmaster play. Containing millions of positions, these opening databases imitate and of course surpass human knowledge and memory of the openings. By accessing these databases of moves, a program will play well over a dozen moves according to a preset routine before it begins to compute for the first time. Without the benefit of this human knowledge in the openings, the programs would be considerably weaker.

Some databases are drawn into service only at the end of the game. These "endgame tablebases," another creation of Ken Thompson, record every possible position with six or fewer pieces (some sets with seven now exist) and their most efficient solutions. With the aid of these oracles we have discovered positions that require over two hundred accurate moves to force a win, a level of complexity previously undreamt of—and still impossible for any human to master.

Fortunately, the two ends—opening research and endgame databases—will never meet, so it is highly unlikely that anyone will ever see a computer play its first move 1.e4 and announce checkmate in 33,520 moves.

And a Child Shall Lead Us

My first experiences with computers were far more pleasant than the more famous encounters we'll come to in a moment. In 1985 I was twenty-two years old and the recently crowned world chess champion. One of my new perks was an early personal computer, one of the few in my hometown of Baku. One couldn't do a great deal with it as I recall, but it fascinated me just the same. One day I received a package in the mail from a stranger named Frederic Friedel, a chess fan and science writer based in Hamburg, Germany. He sent me an admiring note and a floppy disk containing several computer games, including one called Hopper.

Video games weren't yet the phenomenon they had become in the United States, and I enthusiastically took up this new challenge. I spent much of my free time over the next few weeks practicing Hopper and setting ever higher record scores.

A few months later I traveled to Hamburg for a chess event, and I made sure to look up Mr. Friedel at his suburban home. I met his wife and two young sons, Martin, age ten, and Tommy, age three. They made me feel quite at home, and Frederic was eager to show me the latest developments on his own computer. I mentioned that I had completely mastered one of the little games he had sent me.

"You know, I'm the best Hopper player in Baku," I said, omitting any mention of the total lack of competition.

"What's your high score?" he asked.

"Sixteen thousand," I replied, a little surprised that this extraordinary number failed to elicit at least a raised eyebrow.

"Very impressive, but that's not such a big score in this house."

"What? You can beat it?" I asked.

"No, not me."

"Ah, okay, Martin must be the video game whiz."

"No, not Martin."

With a sinking feeling I realized the smile on Frederic's face meant that the household Hopper champion was the three-year-old. I was incredulous. "You can't mean Tommy!" My fears were confirmed when Frederic led his little boy over to the computer and sat him down next to us as the familiar game loaded. Since I was the guest, they let me go first, and I rose to the occasion with a personal best of nineteen thousand points.

My success was short-lived, however, as Tommy took his turn. His little fingers were a blur, and before long the score read twenty thousand, then thirty thousand. I figured I should concede defeat before we sat there watching through dinnertime. My cause was clearly hopeless.

Losing to a little kid at Hopper was easier on my ego than any loss to Karpov, but it still gave me food for thought. How was my country going to compete with a generation of little computer geniuses being raised in the West? Here I was, one of the few people in an entire Soviet city with a computer, handily outperformed by a German toddler. And what about the implications for chess? What if we could improve the way we studied chess the way we used our PCs to write letters and store records? This would be a powerful weapon, one that I shouldn't be the last to have.

But my first opportunity to employ what I learned from this lesson wasn't related to chess. When I signed a sponsorship deal with the computer company Atari, I took as payment over a hundred of their machines to bring back to a youth club in Moscow, the first of its kind in the Soviet Union. We couldn't be left in the Stone Age while Tommy and his nimble-fingered compatriots took over the world.

I had also had the chance to address the other issue with Frederic—how a home computer could be turned into a chess tool. Our conversations led to the creation of the first version of ChessBase, a name now synonymous with professional chess software thanks to the company of the same name that Frederic cofounded in Hamburg. ChessBase was the result of embracing innovation and of being alert to the trends and the possibilities. (And while Martin and Tommy have so far failed to take over the world, both are successful computer design and programming professionals.)

Kasparov vs. Deep Blue

My six-game matches against the IBM supercomputer Deep Blue in 1996 and 1997 received unprecedented attention around the world for a chess event. The official Web site of the 1997 rematch generated Web traffic similar to that of the Atlanta Olympic Games. *Newsweek* ran a cover story titled THE BRAIN'S LAST STAND, and a thousand subplots were developed. Was Deep Blue really artificial intelligence? Was I the defender of humanity? When it was all over, people debated the implications of my initial win in Philadelphia, my loss in New York a year later, and IBM's refusal to play a third, deciding match.

For those who may not remember how the whole thing played out, here's a brief summary. After my first match with Deep Blue in 1996 in Philadelphia received so much publicity, IBM threw its full weight behind a six-game rematch in May 1997 to be held in downtown Manhattan. In 1996, I lost the first game of the match, but after that wake-up call I came back to win three games and easily defeat the computer 4–2. For the rematch IBM claimed "Deeper Blue" was twice as fast and much smarter. They had hired human Grandmasters to work full-time "teaching" the computer by improving its evaluation function.

The media attention for the first game of the rematch was beyond that of a world championship. Over three hundred journalists were accredited, and the five-hundred-seat auditorium sold out at $25 per ticket. Of course I was nervous. Being human, I was unable to ignore all of these distractions, unlike my silicon opponent. But I played well enough to win the first game with white. The second game would, however, change the course of the match, and of human-machine competition.

I've talked about computers and their inability to make long-term plans. They calculate variations in a linear way, examining each move in turn, searching deeper and deeper. Even at Deep Blue's 200 million moves per second, it took it a long time to see far enough ahead to play competent strategic chess. It would occasionally make silly moves no strong human would consider, and it did this in its loss in game one. Game two was an entirely different matter. The machine played with the subtlety of a Karpov, especially at one key moment when I was desperately hoping to gain counterattacking chances. I attempted to sacrifice material for activity, but uncharacteristically for a machine, Deep Blue declined to win material. Instead it played a quiet prophylactic move that ended my hopes, the sort of move no computer had ever before made. Instead of going for a short-term advantage, it closed in for the kill. Faced with a losing position and stunned by the godlike quality of the machine's play, I resigned.

I soon received an even greater shock. It turned out that the final position of the second game was not a losing one for me after all. With its last move the computer had blundered, and I had resigned in a drawn position! It felt like being kicked in the stomach after already being knocked down. When I was shown the drawing line, I realized that I would have continued on against any human. But during the game I couldn't imagine the machine making such a mistake, and I had assumed my position was hopeless. I had completely psyched myself out. My feelings of embarrassment and anger were quickly joined by doubt and suspicion. How could Deep Blue play so fantastically well and then in the same game make such an elementary (for a computer) blunder? My mind began to reel with thoughts about just how far IBM might go to win. Would not billions of dollars in "free favorable publicity"—IBM's words—be worth giving the machine a little human help at a key moment?

Always one to speak my mind, I suggested this possibility in the press conference after the drawn third game. I should have considered that the uproar that followed would only heighten the tension, something that of course had no effect on my opponent. I missed a clear win in the fourth game, and by then I was exhausted and confused. Was something fishy going on, or was Deep Blue really so strong? In the fifth game I again missed good winning chances, so the match remained tied with one win apiece and three draws. Everything was set for a showdown in game six, but looking back today, I see my fate had already been sealed.

It took only nineteen moves for me to resign the worst game of my career and lose the match. I was simply in no condition to play chess by that point, and I made an infantile blunder in the opening. After a few more feeble moves the game and the match were over. I was ashamed of my performance and for letting the mysterious second game get to me.

Worse than the loss of the final decisive game was IBM's blow to the scientific and chess communities by deciding to immediately shut down the Deep Blue project. For half a century chess had been considered a unique field for the comparison of the human and machine minds, of intuition versus calculation. To this day the six games I played with the multimillion-dollar machine are the only ones ever made public. It was as if they had gone to the moon and not taken pictures.

The tragedy of IBM's hurried dismantling of Deep Blue overshadowed their disappointingly questionable behavior during the match. IBM was not only my opponent at the board in the 1997 rematch, but also the organizer of the event. There was so much antagonism, with so many unanswered questions about what was going on behind the scenes, that it was hard to avoid coming up with conspiracy theories. I don't have any proof of foul play, but I feel they didn't prove much either thanks to their decision to terminate their creation. I live in doubt.

Before I am accused of being a sore loser, I will plead guilty to the charge. I hate losing, especially when I don't understand the reason for the loss. When we analyze those six games today, we find that on the whole Deep Blue was inferior to today's PC programs. Only in a few key moments did the IBM computer play extraordinarily subtle moves, moves that even today make one question how they emerged from the same machine that lost game one and blundered at the end of game two.

We have discussed the importance of preparation, and this was another illustration of the incomplete nature of this famous chapter in the man-machine saga. Going into the match, Deep Blue was a complete unknown to me, a black box literally and figuratively. But they could, and did, analyze every one of my games and customize Deep Blue's play to exploit that advantage.

The closed nature of the contest created the potential for human interference, although in the pre-Enron era it sounded like paranoid folly to suggest that a corporate giant might resort to subterfuge to gain publicity and a huge surge in its stock price. Despite these remaining sour feelings, I was amazed at the enormous appeal the match clearly had for the general public. I knew I wanted to continue the adventure, although in the future the environment would need to be much more open and scientific.

If You Can't Beat 'Em, Join 'Em

My enthusiasm for finding new ways to use computer technology to promote the game of chess did not disappear when IBM pulled the plug on Deep Blue. In 1998 I turned to a new experiment dedicated to enabling humans to fight along with machines instead of against them.

Grandmasters play chess by combining experience with intuition, backed up with calculation and study. Computers play chess by brute calculation; their "study" consists of a gigantic database of opening moves. At present there is a rough equilibrium between these methods; the best computers play at around the same strength as the best humans. As microprocessors have got faster, humans have learned new tricks to expose the weaknesses of computer play. Inevitably the machines must win, but there is still a long way to go before a human on his or her best day is unable to defeat the best computer.

The concept of Advanced Chess illustrates the costs and benefits of human + computer collaboration. I developed this game as a way of answering the elusive but fascinating question, what would a combination of human intuition and computer calculation produce on the chessboard? Would they combine into an invincible centaur or an uncoordinated Frankenstein's monster? In June 1998, with two powerful computers at their sides, two Grandmasters, Veselin Topalov and I, faced off across the board in the first match of its kind.

Although I had prepared for the unusual format, our six-game match was full of strange sensations. We all use computer programs in our analysis and training, so we know what they are capable of and what their weaknesses are. But having one available during play was as disturbing as it was exciting. Being able to access a database of a few million games meant we didn't have to strain our memories nearly as much in the opening. But since we both had equal access to the same database, the advantage still came down to creating a new move at some point, and making sure it was better than what had been played before.

In the middle game, having a computer running meant never having to worry about making a tactical blunder. We could concentrate more on deep planning instead of the precise calculations that take up so much of our time in regular games. Again, since we were both using computers, it was a matter of how well we used them to check our plans and whose plan was more effective. As when I played against Deep Blue, there would be no way back if I made an error. The machine would not forgive any mistakes by making one of its own in return.

It was difficult to find the best way to utilize the machine's abilities. I felt I was in a race to check the validity of the computer's evaluation. It gives its opinion instantly, but its recommendation changes as its analysis goes deeper and deeper. Just as a good Formula One driver really knows his own car, so did we have to learn the way the computer program worked. There is a strong impulse to unquestioningly follow the machine's evaluation if the move it recommends looks like something the computer would usually play well. That's a dangerous habit.

Despite the human + machine formula, my games with Topalov were far from perfect, mostly due to the unforgiving clock and the intense time pressure we were under. Toward the end, we had no time on our clocks to consult the machines for more than a few seconds. Putting that flaw aside, the results were interesting. Just a month earlier I had defeated the Bulgarian 4–0 in a match of regular rapid chess. Our Advanced Chess match finished in a 3–3 draw.

An important benefit of Advanced Chess is that the computer

creates a log of every variation the players examined during play. This leaves a diary of the players' thoughts throughout the game, which is both fascinating for online spectators and immensely valuable as a training tool. Normally it is forbidden to take any notes during a game, but in Advanced Chess we provide a complete map of the path the game took through the players' minds.

The experiment continued in León in later years with other players, and in 2005 the ethos of Advanced Chess found its true home on the Internet. The online site Playchess.com hosted what they called a "freestyle" chess tournament in which anyone could compete in teams with other players or computers—whichever they prefer. Lured by the substantial prize money, groups of strong Grandmasters working with several computers at the same time entered the competition.

At first, the results seemed predictable. The teams of human plus machine totally dominated even the strongest computers. The mighty chess machine Hydra, which is hardware-based like Deep Blue, was no match for a strong human using a relatively weak laptop. Human strategic guidance combined with the tactical acuity of a computer was invincible.

The surprise came at the conclusion of the event. The winner was revealed to be not a Grandmaster with a souped-up machine, but a pair of amateur American chess players using three computers at the same time. Their skill at manipulating and "coaching" their computers to look deeply into positions effectively counteracted the superior understanding of their Grandmaster opponents. Weak human + machine + superior process was greater than a strong computer and, remarkably, greater than a strong human + machine with an inferior process.

The "freestyle" winners had taken advantage of superior coordination of their contrasting methods and strengths. They understood their tools—human and machine—and figured out how best to get the most from them. A manager might say they built an effective team from a group of individuals with disparate skill sets. An army commander would recognize that a well-coordinated force will almost always triumph over a numerically superior enemy who lacks organization. A company with an efficient management structure, or assembly line, will often have better margins than a larger, less agile competitor. Process is critical, especially since its benefits multiply with each cycle.

Staying Out of the Comfort Zone

Opposite pairs working in harmony: this has become a theme of our quest to perfect decision-making. Calculation and evaluation. Patience and opportunism, intuition and analysis, style and objectivity. At the performance level these elements come together in management and vision, strategy and tactics, planning and reaction. Success comes from balancing these forces and harnessing their inherent power.

And as we've seen again and again in this book, the only consistent method for achieving such a balance is to constantly seek to avoid our comfort zone. It's a bad habit to become overreliant on one skill or way of doing things just because it has in the past worked well for you. It's better to throw yourself off-balance, as Topalov and I did in that first game of Advanced Chess. One of the lessons I took away from that match I think about almost every day: the one time you are surely learning something is when you are nervously attempting something new, even if it is simply solving a routine problem in a novel way. If you want an illustration of how deeply you are set in your routines, try brushing your teeth left-handed, or putting on your trousers left leg first. Our mental routines are no less ingrained—and they have more profound consequences.

Engaging with the weakest points in our game and drilling down so we really understand them is the best and fastest way to improve. Working to become a universal player—someone who can defend as well as attack and is at home in any type of position—may not always have an obvious immediate benefit, especially if you are in a specialized field. But in my experience working toward a universal style creates a rising tide that lifts all boats. Gaining experience in one area improves our overall abilities in unexpected, often inexplicable ways.

I was lucky in that I was virtually forced by Anatoly Karpov to become a more positional, strategic player. It was sink or swim for me: either I broadened my style and my understanding or I wouldn't be able to beat him. The situation is not so clear for most people. We can go through our day-to-day lives without changing our habits and nothing terrible will happen to us. The problem is that it is also highly unlikely anything *at all* will happen to us—including good things. Successfully avoiding challenges is not an accomplishment to be proud of.

When I was in the fifth grade, the greatest mystery that school held for me was drawing. It seemed like an occult science; I just couldn't do it, and to this day I'm lousy at it. Instead of working at drawing as I did my other subjects, I—cleverly I thought—convinced my mother to do my drawing homework. She was quite good; in fact, she was good enough to catch the attention of my teacher with a fine picture she made of a bird in a tree. I could no sooner have drawn that myself than I could have painted the *Mona Lisa*. My teacher asked me if I would be interested in entering a drawing competition, in which I would have to perform in front of judges, not at home. If you think this is the end of the story, you haven't realized how proud and competitive I was even then.

Instead of confessing, I spent the next few weeks at home training myself to draw the picture of the bird exactly as my mother had. I spent hours on it, reproducing it line by line as if memorizing a chemical formula. Eventually I could manage a quite reasonable facsimile of the bird. Sweating nervously at the competition, I produced a creature that was almost identical to my mother's original. I have no doubt that that bird was and is the only thing I could draw in the world.

Of course now I wish I had done my drawing homework myself and actually learned to appreciate and cultivate the skill it requires. But even if I can't draw a picture, I did benefit from the lesson that experience offered. I stepped out of my comfort zone and pushed a bit at the boundaries of what I thought I could do. And it wasn't such a bad bird, after all.

It has long been fashionable to talk about left-brain and right-brain activities, even left-brained and right-brained people. But it doesn't require a discussion of brain science to understand how indulging our creative side and letting our minds wander in artistic pursuits can be enormously helpful in breaking us out of our problem-solving routines.

The great physicist Richard Feynman offers an inspiring example of a brilliant man who pushed the boundaries and refused to be defined by his achievements in one particular area. When Robert Oppenheimer was in charge of the Manhattan Project, which produced the atomic bomb, he described Feynman as "the most brilliant young physicist here." But he was also the greatest troublemaker. He saw everything as a challenge, as a puzzle to be solved. Feynman enjoyed picking the locks in the top-secret offices of Los Alamos just to see if he could. He became a serious amateur painter and musician and loved to perform as a drummer at Brazilian carnival celebrations.

I have no doubt that Feynman's free spirit and playful mind were assets to his scientific work, not detriments. In his popular books he insisted that science was a living subject, not just a cold set of formulas. He excelled in combining techniques and transforming a difficult problem into a comparable one that was easier to solve. This skill was directly related to his inclination to stay open to new ideas in every aspect of his life.

Today our society places great emphasis on specialization and focus. Students used to go off to university with the idea of broadening themselves; now it has become a mostly vocational experience. Students use higher education as a means to develop a skill that will make them attractive to employers. We place so much emphasis on being good at what we do that we fail to realize that getting better at what we do might be best achieved by getting better at other—and wildly different—things.

It sounds strange to say that being a better artist might make me a stronger chess player or that listening to classical music can make you a more effective manager. And yet this is exactly the sort of thing that Feynman had in mind when he said that being a drummer made him a better physicist. When we regularly challenge ourselves with something new—even something not obviously related to our immediate goals—we build cognitive and emotional "muscles" that make us more effective in every way. If we can overcome our fear of speaking in public, or of submitting a poem to a magazine, or learning a new language, confidence will flow into every area of our lives. Don't get so caught up in "what I do" that you stop being a curious human being. Your greatest strength is the ability to absorb and synthesize patterns, methods, and information. Intentionally inhibiting that ability by focusing too narrowly is not only a crime, but one with few rewards.

My relationship with computers over the years has been contentious, but I readily acknowledge they have had a major impact on the way I think. Both playing against them and using them as an analytical tool forced me to recognize flaws in my decision-making. Like any tool, computers extend our reach and present us with new ways of solving old problems. They also present us with an entirely new set of problems, but this can be a blessing in disguise. Solving new problems is what keeps us moving forward as individuals and as a society, so don't back down.

CHAPTER 14

INTUITION

We Know More Than We Understand

Agatha Christie said of intuition, "You can't ignore it and you can't explain it." But we don't need a pat explanation to recognize how important it is and investigate how we can develop ours to its maximum potential.

Despite the efforts of psychologists and neurologists, human thought is still best described by metaphor, poetry, and other literary devices we use to express what we do not fully understand. Not being a poet, I will keep my focus on the more practical mission of understanding what we might call executive brain management.

Aldous Huxley, ignoring Freud and writing long before the invention of brain scans, defined experience as "a matter of sensibility and intuition, of seeing and hearing the significant things, of paying attention at the right moments, of understanding and coordinating. Experience is not what happens to a man; it is what a man does with what happens to him."

All along this has been a book about taking action—about playing an active and focused role in our own development. Because the truth is that we can't sit around and expect wisdom to accumulate along with gray hair. I've talked about the importance of learning from your mistakes, but in truth that's almost a passive act, at least in comparison to actively going out in search of new experiences that will teach you new and extraordinary things. Learning from our mistakes is the least we should ask from ourselves. To get more we must demand it and go looking for it.

Intuition is where it all comes together: it is the indispensable product of our experience, our knowledge, and our will to know and do more. It's my opinion that, contrary to popular belief, we cannot truly experience the spark of intuition in a field in which we have little practical knowledge. The first-time chess player who makes the right move based on his feeling for a certain piece is probably experiencing luck, not intuition. But when a knowledgeable player finds the best move simply present in his mind without combing through hundreds of variations, that's the power of intuition. Even the vaguest of hunches is based on something tangible—some knowledge, even though it may be buried deep below our conscious mind. A positive impression of a new co-worker can stem from a deeply embedded recollection of another's voice, face, or name. That we cannot explain or understand it does not mean that this powerful force of recollected knowledge does not exist.

Discussing the complexity of human intuition reminds me of the dilemma that was summed up by the onetime head of the Spanish royal household, Sabino Fernández Campo, who said, "What I can tell you is not interesting, and what is interesting I cannot tell you." So instead of theory I had best stick to concrete examples that might help me convince you to have more faith in your instincts. This is the essential element that cannot be measured by any analysis or device, and I believe it's at the heart of success in all things: the power of intuition and the ability to harness and use it like a master.

Intuition vs. Analysis

After I wrote a series of short newspaper articles on the world champions who came before me, I became obsessed with the idea of analyzing in depth how the game has changed over the decades and how its development has been pushed along by its greatest practitioners. I had in mind a biography of chess itself told through the careful analysis of the greatest and most influential games. This project, which has taken up a large part of my life for the past three years, came to life as a series of books titled *My Great Predecessors*.

During my work on *My Great Predecessors* I gained not just deeper respect for the achievements of the world champions, but a greater admiration for the ways that the game of chess can bring out the best in the human mind. Few activities are as taxing to our faculties as a professional chess tournament. Memory is in overdrive, rapid calculation is essential, the outcome hangs on every move, and a match goes on for hour after hour, day after day, all with the world watching. It is the ideal scenario for mental and physical meltdown.

When I began to analyze the games of my world champion forebears, I was, therefore, prepared to be a little forgiving. Not in my analysis, but in my attitude toward their mistakes. Here I was in the twenty-first century, standing on the shoulders of giants with gigahertz of chess processing power at my fingertips. With these advantages and the objectivity of hindsight I shouldn't judge my predecessors too harshly, I told myself, even as I would hope, years from now, to receive some forgiveness for the mistakes I made in the heat of competition.

An important part of the project was to collect all the relevant analysis that had been done on these games before, especially the published analyses of the players themselves and their contemporaries. The principal theme of the series is to illustrate the evolution of the game, so the commentary of the time is as valuable as the games themselves in revealing the mentality of the players of each era.

One would assume that the analyst, working in the calm of his study and with unlimited time to move the pieces, would have a much easier job than the players themselves. Hindsight is twenty-twenty, after all, or so we are told. To my surprise I found that when other top players in the precomputer age (before 1995, roughly) wrote about games in magazines and newspaper columns, they often made more mistakes in their annotations than the players had made at the board. Hindsight, it seemed, was badly in need of bifocals. Even when the players themselves published an analysis of their own games, they often were less perceptive than they had been while actually playing the game.

Here's an example of how a herd of experts failed to see, decade after decade, how human intuition triumphed in the crucial moment.

Game seven was the decisive encounter of the 1894 world championship match between the fifty-seven-year-old champion Wilhelm Steinitz and his young German challenger, twenty-five-year-old Emanuel Lasker. The players had split the first four games two wins apiece, followed by two draws. Then came what the commentators at the time predicted was lucky number seven. Which of the players would be the lucky one is perhaps not yet clear to this day.

Lasker misplayed early on with the white pieces, and Steinitz exploited his chances so effectively that he had a clean pair of extra pawns when the smoke cleared at move twenty. If a Grandmaster today resigned in such a position, it wouldn't provoke much surprise among the viewing public. Play was much less precise a century ago, and of course Lasker had nothing to lose by playing on. At the very least he would tire out his elder opponent for the next encounter. Already a shrewd psychologist of the chessboard, Lasker likely hoped that the sheer bravado of his decision to press on would disturb the dogmatic veteran.

Most analyses of the game at the time went something like this: Steinitz, as black, had a clearly winning position. Lasker launched a desperate attack against black's king, sacrificing a piece. Still winning but now under some pressure, Steinitz committed a suicidal mistake that cost him the game. The shock of blundering so badly affected Steinitz so much that he went on to lose the next four games in a row and the world title. At least that's the official story.

But there's another way to see the game. The revised story would go something like this. Steinitz had an objectively winning position—but he made a few errors, and those errors allowed Lasker to launch a risky but brilliant attack, making the position quite complicated. The challenger's subsequent play and piece sacrifice set many practical problems for black. Under constant pressure, Steinitz failed to defend accurately and lost. Steinitz's final mistake came in a position where he was already losing. The psychological blow of being outplayed despite his superficially simple and winning position stunned Steinitz, and he was unable to recover in the match. More than his self-confidence had been shaken by the loss. The principles of sound and logical chess that Steinitz held so dear had seemingly betrayed him. He was sure he had been winning and he had played according to his philosophy. And yet he had lost.

The result may have been the same either way, but there is a world of difference in getting the story right. A veteran master such as Steinitz would not have been so damaged by a mere oversight, no matter how grave its consequences. All chess players know "chess blindness" can strike anyone at any time. What shook Steinitz was that he *hadn't* blundered. The game had been taken out of his grip by the young Lasker's energetic play. We can tell from the way the game progressed that Lasker could not have seen all the way to the end of every variation, but he didn't have to. His intuition told him he would have good practical chances.

How could so many strong players miss in analysis what Lasker sensed during the game? Even Lasker himself never challenged the official story in his later observations, but his intuition had led him unfailingly and correctly during the game. It turns out that this is not at all unusual, even a century later—in my own games and analysis as well as others'. For starters, it is impossible for the analyst sitting in his comfortable study to replicate the level of concentration reached during a game. The freedom we have in analysis to move the pieces around can be a crutch that leads us to use our eyes instead of our minds. When seated at the board, we have no choice but to focus our full powers.

Over and over again these legendary figures, at the most crucial moments of their careers, intuitively found the best moves. Competitive pressure made them push deeper. Those of us who come along later and apply all our skills and knowledge to the analysis of the moves aren't under that pressure. Some of our senses are turned off and we become like a sighted person who is midway through learning braille: we perceive the information that's in front of us—under our fingertips—but we can't fully understand it. The things we usually think of as advantages—having more time to think and analyze, having more information at our disposal—can short-circuit what matters even more: our intuition.

How Long Is Long Enough?

This example is not intended to encourage you to blindly follow your gut instinct, or to rely indiscriminately on simple first impressions. As we've seen over and over, diligent study and the gathering of knowledge about what came before in chess are essential to becoming a successful competitor. What I do want to illustrate is the power of concentration and instinct. The biggest problem I see among people who want to excel in chess—and in business and in life in general—is not trusting these instincts enough. Too often they rely on having all the information, which then forces them to a conclusion. This effectively reduces them to the role of a microprocessor and guarantees that their intuition will remain dormant.

Everything comes at a cost. Challenging yourself in new ways inevitably leads to a few failures. At times your instincts will all point in one direction, and that direction is a dead end. So you err, you learn, you make fewer mistakes, you gain more confidence, you trust your instincts more readily and you continue the cycle. The result of trying anything is either failure or success. If you wish to succeed, you must brave the risk of failure.

When the dot-com bubble began to expand in the 1990s, it set off the alarm bells of just about every "old economy" analyst. Surely this couldn't be real; companies without revenue simply were not worth billions of dollars of market capital. Five years later, after the markets had plummeted and thousands of companies had gone bankrupt, it was easy to say that those sober analysts had been correct all along. They trusted their intuition and stayed well away from the wild side of the tech market while so many others had closed the traditional playbook, jumped all the way in, and got badly burned.

But were the conservative doomsayers really right? Sure, it takes discipline to resist jumping into the pool when all the other kids are doing it, but after a while it can become a habit and you never jump in at all. Some credit should be given to the few who played it well, whose fine intuitive senses told them to first go in and second just how long to stay in. For all the famous disaster stories—and my own dot-com venture is somewhere on that list—plenty of investors ran into the burning building, filled their pockets with Internet gold, and got out before it collapsed. The conservative crowd was right on the fundamentals, but that didn't mean there wasn't money to be made by a savvy few.

Any discipline in which access to information is nearly unlimited but time is a major factor has a strong intuitive element. Stock analysts search for visual patterns in stock charts, shapes such as "teacups" and "rising wedges," the way chess players look for checkmating patterns. Intuition tells us not just what and how, but also when. I can ponder my move for ten seconds, ten minutes, or one hour. A well-developed intuition lets me know when I have reached a critical juncture that requires more time and special attention. As they develop, our instincts—our intuitive senses—become labor-saving and time-saving devices; they literally cut down the time it takes to make a proper evaluation and act. You can collect and analyze new information forever without ever making a decision. Something has to tell you when the law of diminishing returns is kicking in. And that something is intuition.

The Perils of Ignoring a Trend

The pattern recognition that chess players rely on is essential in every walk of life. In every new situation we have to determine whether what we are dealing with is a trend or something unique. Detecting trends, preferably before anyone else, is often based on intuition and intangible elements. Has it happened before? Will it develop the same way this time?

Figuring out whether an event is a one-off, a new trend, or an old trend in new clothes is especially important in the political world. During every election season the media reports a half dozen "new paradigms," although few turn out to be both new and relevant. In the U.S. presidential election in 2004 the Democrats looked back at Al Gore's defeat in 2000 and chose the wrong man as John Kerry's running mate.

The choice of John Edwards might have made sense in the Kerry campaign headquarters, but if you looked at the trends that were evident from the country's electoral map, it made no sense at all. Bush had dominated the South in the 2000 election, and there was no reason to believe that Edwards could carry even a single Southern state for the Democrats.

On Election Day 2004 the Democratic "blues" again lost the entire South; they even lost Edwards's home state of North Carolina by the same thirteen points Gore had lost it by in 2000. To further add insult to injury, the Democrats had spent heavily in North Carolina to make it a respectable loss and save face for Edwards.

The Democrats chose to believe that Gore's loss in the South had been an aberration. Going by a "material, time, quality" analysis, this led them on the path to disaster. They were punished for their mismanagement of financial resources, their failure to recognize a trend quickly enough, and for their poor choice of battlefield. If they had properly interpreted the loss of the entire South in 2000 as the trend it clearly turned out to be, they might have selected Dick Gephardt instead of Edwards. The addition of the Midwestern stalwart would have created a good chance of flipping Iowa and Missouri and changing their eighteen electoral votes from red to blue, providing Kerry with a 269–268 victory over Bush despite the loss of Ohio.

Gore's near miss in 2000 lulled the Kerry campaign into believing nothing essential had changed in 2004. In one way they were correct. The only change in the 2004 electoral map from that of 2000 was that the Democrats swapped the gain of New Hampshire for the loss of New Mexico and Iowa. But more than anything, the Kerry campaign had lost sight of the point: they refought the losing battles of 2000 instead of seeking out new tactical advantages. They looked at the 2000 map and chose to fight the trend it represented instead of looking for new opportunities, such as going after the Midwest with a vice-presidential candidate from Missouri.

To be fair, the point is that nobody knows for sure when a change is a trend until it's already too late. Political operatives and marketing executives are paid a lot of money to process the available information and make the right choices. Inevitably, somebody has to be wrong. In the 2006 U.S. midterm elections, for example, both the Democrats and the Republicans bet everything on the issue of the war in Iraq. Most polls showed it was a loser issue for Republicans and the Bush administration, but Karl Rove and other GOP strategists were convinced they had enough votes in key races to keep control of Congress. However, the tough talk and "support the troops" rhetoric that was so successful for Republicans in 2004 was a failure in 2006. Even some moderate Republicans who had stopped supporting Bush on Iraq were swept from office by the antiwar tide that some Republicans had underestimated as just a wave.

Distinguishing between an anomaly and a movement can't be done with polls and data alone. We have to focus our attention on any new event and extend all our senses. What exactly makes it new? In what ways is it like something we have seen before? How has the environment changed? If we can answer these questions, we will have an excellent chance of knowing whether a single snowflake is about to become a blizzard.

CHAPTER 15

CRISIS POINT

Everything is condensed into one single moment.
It decides our life.

—FRANZ KAFKA

One Single Moment

What would intimidate you more, being told "Solve this problem" or being told "Find out if there's a problem"? Solving problems could be described as easy compared to figuring out whether there is a problem in the first place. It's hard to say we're lucky when we face a crisis, but we at least have the luxury of knowing that action is called for—of being forced to move. The truest tests of skill and intuition come when everything looks quiet and we aren't sure what to do, or if we should do anything at all.

Anyone who has sat for a multiple-choice exam knows the most feared option is "none of the above." Suddenly it's open-ended. Maybe there is no solution at all, who knows? Try this short mathematics test, which won't require a calculator.

$13 \times 63 = ?$

(a) 109

(b) 819

(c) 8,109

No trouble at all, of course. The answer is found by a simple process of elimination. Our intuition tells us instantly that we don't have to calculate anything. But if we add "(d) none of the above," we have to do the work and solve the equation no matter how obviously wrong answers (a) and (c) are.

We touched on this earlier, in our discussion of composed chess puzzles. In these puzzles, you are presented with a position and stipulations. "White to checkmate in three moves" is precise. "White to play and win" is more open-ended, but in both cases we know before we start that there is something to be found. Relieved of the need to evaluate and be vigilant, we turn the matter over to the problem-solving section of our brain.

In such cases, we can perform these tasks with remarkable efficiency. In 1987, I was invited to a special reception in Frankfurt held by Atari. All of their managers were there, and the master of ceremonies was the head of their German division, Alwin Stumpf. It was an informal and entertaining evening where we discussed politics as well as chess and computers. (In fact, I earned the friendly condescension of most everyone with my prediction that as a consequence of the changes in the USSR, the Berlin Wall would soon fall, perhaps in as little as five years. "A fine chess player," everyone said, "but he doesn't know anything about politics!" As it turns out, my forecast allowed three years too many.)

After the banquet was finished, Herr Stumpf took the microphone and grandly pronounced that we were about to see something extraordinary: he had seen me perform an amazing feat on television and now I was going to do it in person. I had no idea what he had in mind when he pointed to a long table on the other side of the room that we had passed on the way in. Stumpf explained that the table held a dozen chessboards, each set up to reflect a position from a historic game of chess, spanning 150 years of play. In front of each board, a facedown card listed the date, place, and names of the players. I was to be tested to see if I could identify each game by looking at the position on the board. Stumpf walked over to the table and invited me to join him so the challenge could begin.

When I remained in my seat, a look of fear crossed his face—he was clearly worried that he had gravely insulted me with his little surprise. I said, "I'm honored you are interested in understanding the human mind, but I hope you will forgive me if I stay seated." Stumpf looked forlorn. I was going to ruin his big moment! But then I said that I couldn't help glancing at the boards as we had walked into the hall and that I would like to try to name all the games from here, in my chair across the room. So one by one I named the players, the tournament, and even the next move of each game represented on the dozen boards.

The effect was satisfactorily jaw-dropping for the guests, and looking back on it, I try to forgive myself a youthful display of the dramatic. What I did not explain, and likely didn't even realize at the time myself, was that they had made it easy for me. Not with the game selection, because not all of the positions were even taken from world-famous encounters. But of course each position they had selected was from the critical moment of each game. No self-respecting chess fan would select a nondescript position from a deservedly forgotten game when there are so many fascinating and famous positions to choose from.

It was enough to know that since the first position was the key moment of a known game from history, the others were likely similar. Had the positions appeared uninteresting or trivial, I would perhaps have assumed the participants had been playing some casual games before I arrived. When I glanced at the boards, I quickly recognized that I didn't have to evaluate the positions; all I had to do was look them up in my memory.

Knowing a solution is at hand is a huge advantage; it's like not having a "none of the above" option. Anyone with reasonable competence and adequate resources can solve a puzzle when it is presented as something to be solved. We can skip the subtle evaluations and move directly to plugging in possible solutions until we hit upon a promising one. Uncertainty is far more challenging. Instead of immediately looking for solutions to the crisis, we have to maintain a constant state of asking, "Is there a crisis forming?"

Detecting a Crisis Before It's a Crisis

Detecting a crisis in the making is a separate skill from solving one. (Here I'm distinguishing crisis from catastrophe; it doesn't take much skill or intuition to realize when things have gone horribly wrong.) In a 1959 speech in Indianapolis, John F. Kennedy famously observed that the Chinese word for "crisis" is composed of two characters, one meaning danger and the other meaning opportunity. Though this turns out not to be literally true, it is a poetic and memorable way to illustrate a useful concept.

I was somewhat surprised to discover that the English definition of the word is also illustrative. From its common usage we might assume it means something like "disaster," which needs no further synonyms. But in fact, *crisis* really means a turning point, a critical moment when the stakes are high and the outcome uncertain. It also implies a point of no return. This signifies both danger and opportunity, so Kennedy's speech was accurate where it mattered.

Great success with minimal risk of failure is a goal held by many, especially in the modern political and commercial environment. It may even be achievable—if you have many advantages to start with, the way an heir to a fortune does when he enters a business. And it would be pleasant, if boring, to forever take our boat down calm and straight streams, never encountering rapids or bends in the course. But for most of us, avoiding crises entirely—which often only means postponing them or, worse, ignoring them altogether—carries a great risk of its own.

Instead, real success depends on detecting, evaluating, and controlling risk. Of these three things, detection is often the most important and always the most difficult. Important because without it, instead of controlling risk we end up fighting to survive when the crisis hits. Difficult because it requires alertness to the most subtle changes.

World champion Boris Spassky once observed, "The best indicator of a chess player's form is his ability to sense the climax of the game." It is virtually impossible to play the best move every single turn, because accuracy comes at the expense of time and vice versa. But if we can detect the key moments, we can make our best decisions when they matter most. The moves we make on the chessboard are far from equal in importance, and you must rely on intuition to tell you that here, at this precise moment, you need to spend some extra time because the game may hinge on this one decision.

Apart from its merit as an indicator of good or poor form, the ability to detect these crisis points is a gauge of overall strength in a chess player—and in a decision-maker. The greatest players are distinguished by their ability to recognize crucial factors that are both specific and general. Analysis of past games illustrates this well, despite the challenges I referred to earlier of comprehending today what was going through the mind of someone one hundred years ago. We can't be positive that Lasker knew a certain move was the climax of the game, but we can tell from analyzing his play when he found the best moves and when he didn't. Usually we also know how much time the players invested in each move.

Learning from a Crisis

Chateaubriand wrote, "Moments of crisis produce a redoubling of life in man." These are the times when we are tested, when we develop our skills and our senses. Take a moment to look back on your last crisis and how you handled it. If you cannot recall a recent crisis in your life, even one successfully averted, you are either lucky, bored, or both.

It is not pure bravado that leads some individuals to constantly push themselves and those around them to the breaking point in pursuit of conflict. Times of conflict can create opportunities that would never otherwise exist. Provoking a crisis requires perfect timing if you plan to survive the consequences. You can have the other key factors on your side—material and quality—and still be ruined if you misjudge the prevailing environment.

A Final Chess Story: The Crisis in Seville

I can look back at my chess career and pick out more than a few crisis points, but only one Mount Everest. I would like to share the tale to investigate the means I used in winning the most important game of my life.

After winning the world championship in 1985, I had little time to savor the taste of victory. The traditional cycle called for a title defense every three years. During that time the challenger would be produced by rigorous qualification through regional tournaments, giant "interzonal" tournaments, and finally a series of candidate matches. This was so grueling that a challenger in the final was undoubtably a worthy contender. In fact, since the qualification system began in 1950—when it was just a single tournament—only two players who reached a world championship match have failed to become champion eventually.

This process was interrupted in my case, however, thanks to the rematch clause, a defunct rule that FIDE resurrected in the seventies under Soviet pressure to favor Karpov. If the champion lost, he had the right to an automatic rematch a year later with no qualification process. This rule had been abolished after Botvinnik, who had poor scores in world championship matches but was devastating in the rematches, used it to reclaim the title he lost to Smyslov in 1957 and then Tal in 1960.

To avoid the same fate I would have to beat Karpov again in 1986. Bear in mind that we had already played the longest championship match in history in 1984–85, then played another grueling match in 1985, in which I took the title. I narrowly won the rematch in 1986, but the ordeal was still not over. The qualification cycle had started on schedule in 1985 despite our canceled marathon match, the rescheduled match, and the rematch. This meant that I was due to face the scheduled challenger in 1987, exactly a year after beating Karpov. And who would my opponent be this time? Karpov.

Evading the main qualification process, my nemesis had been dropped into a "superfinal" and had duly demolished the leading contender, Andrei Sokolov. In October 1987 we sat down in Seville, Spain, to begin our fourth world championship match in three years. If I had thought I was tired of looking at Karpov back in 1984, I was really sick of him by now. At least this time there were no more tricks. If I won this match, I wouldn't have to see him or any other title challenger for another three years. Apart from the freedom from the exhausting battle of the match itself, this also meant not having to endure the months of intense preparation that always precede such a match.

Must-Win Strategy

Perhaps my eagerness to avoid playing another match with Karpov for another three years is what led to such a turbulent start to our match in Seville. Four of the first eight games were decisive, two wins each and four draws. I was disappointed with my uneven play and my inability to put any distance between us. After a terrible Karpov blunder, I won the eleventh game from a dubious position to take the lead for the first time in the match, scheduled for twenty-four games. After four draws Karpov won the sixteenth game to draw even. At this point I began to think only of my title. A 12–12 score—a drawn match—would allow me to retain the championship. Hardly the convincing victory I had hoped for to end our marathon, but beggars cannot be choosers, and, more important, a draw would give me three years of peace. I went into defensive mode and stopped pressing him. A stretch of six quite uneventful draws followed, setting up a showdown in the final two games.

I didn't want to push and Karpov didn't have the energy to do so. Two more draws seemed the most logical result. Members of my analysis team thought so too. They didn't tell me about their side wagers until after the match had ended, but Grandmaster Zurab Azmaiparashvili made a bet against Grandmaster Josef Dorfman on the last two games, giving away phenomenal odds for any outcome other than two more draws.

It would have done my heart a great deal of good had Dorfman lost his bet, but unfortunately the string of draws would end at six. After a tough, prolonged defense I suffered one of the worst hallucinations of my career and blundered to a loss in game twenty-three. Suddenly Karpov was up by a point and was only a draw away from taking back the crown he had lost to me two years earlier. The very next day after this catastrophe, I had to take the white pieces into a must-win game twenty-four. Caissa, the goddess of chess, had punished me for my conservative play, for betraying my nature. I would not be allowed to hold on to my title without winning a game in the second half of the match.

Only once before in chess history had the champion won a final game to retain his title. With his back against the wall, Emanuel Lasker beat Carl Schlechter in the last game of their match in 1910. The win allowed Lasker to draw the match and keep his title for a further eleven years. The Austrian Schlechter had, like Karpov, a reputation as a defensive wizard. In fact, his uncharacteristically aggressive play in the final game against Lasker has led some historians to believe that the rules of that particular match required him to win by two points.

In 1985 the situation had been reversed. I had gone into the final game leading by a point, and Karpov needed to win to tie the match and save the title he had held since 1975. As discussed in chapter 2, in that decisive game Karpov started out with an all-or-nothing attack. At the critical moment he was betrayed by his own instincts and failed to find the best moves. He had started out the game playing in my direct style only to slow down to his own more cautious approach in midstream, with predictably poor results.

When preparing for my turn on the other side of this situation, I recalled that critical encounter. What strategy should I employ with the white pieces in this must-win final game? There was more to think about than game twenty-three and game twenty-four, of course. These were also games 119 and 120 between us, an extraordinary number of top-level encounters between the same two players, all played in a span of thirty-nine months. It felt like one long match, with this final game in December 1987 the climax of what we had started in September 1984. My plan for the final game had to consider not only what I would like best but what my opponent would like least. And what could be more annoying for Karpov than my turning the tables and playing like Karpov?

Errors on Both Sides

Had I not battled against Karpov for 119 games, I would have been incapable of surviving the all-important 120th. The loss of game twenty-three itself had the potential to be crushing, and I had less than twenty-four hours to prepare what could be my last game as world chess champion. The "secret" of my preparation? Playing cards with my team and getting a good five or six hours of sleep.

The aggregate score of our world championship marathon was sixteen wins apiece and eighty-seven draws. Victory in this 120th game would mean not only winning this match but taking the lead in our overall score. So why cards and sleep instead of opening preparation? After 119 games with Karpov there was nothing my team and I were going to uncover in a few hours of anxious analysis. We decided on a basic strategy, nothing more than that. The rest of the time was better spent recovering my nervous and physical energy for the battle ahead. This might sound strange given my typically obsessive preparation, but it was a simple matter of allocation of resources. Here, I would be best served to trade time for quality. The strategy I had chosen would require not explosive energy but a slow burn.

The magnificent Teatro Lope de Vega was packed for game twenty-four. The entire game was shown live on Spanish television. The usual pregame murmur of the audience had been replaced by a low roar. I was later told that the excited Spanish radio and television commentators sounded as if they were covering the final round of a heavyweight boxing match, which in a sense they were.

The arbiter started my clock and I pushed my c-pawn forward two squares, just as I had done eight times previously in the match. The difference would come in the next few moves as I kept my center pawns back and instead developed on the flanks, carefully avoiding a do-or-die battle. I opened slowly, even a little passively, to keep as many pieces as possible on the board. This technique would put psychological pressure on Karpov, despite his expertise in such maneuvers. With no clear, forcing continuations he would constantly be tempted to simplify and exchange pieces even at the cost of a slightly inferior position. Obviously with fewer pieces on the board the level of complexity would drop, reducing the chances of a decisive result, but as long as I could put a sufficiently high "quality price tag" on these exchanges, I felt I was getting good value.

My slow-cook method had the additional advantage of getting Karpov into serious time trouble. With the stakes so high he was being extra-cautious, taking valuable minutes to double-check moves he would normally make quickly. As the game progressed, Karpov exchanged half the pieces, but his position was still under uncomfortable pressure. He was so close to equalizing on every move, but he couldn't quite get his head above water; in the meantime his clock was becoming a factor.

Seeing a chance to play for an attack, I moved my knight to the central e5 square, offering a pawn. Karpov took the bait and grabbed the pawn, a temptation that could have led to disaster. And he had to play quickly now, as it was still a long way to move forty, when, by the rules then in force, the game would be adjourned and more time added before continuation the next day. (Today, mostly due to the players using computers to help them analyze, such adjournments are obsolete.)

I exchanged rooks, leaving me with queen, knight, and bishop against his queen and two knights. He had an extra pawn, but I had seen a tactical possibility that would give me a powerful attack. His pieces were dangerously uncoordinated, and his king was vulnerable. If I could penetrate into his position with my queen, I could exploit both of these factors at the same time. The question was where to move my queen on move thirty-three. Karpov could only wait, knowing he would have to reply almost immediately or he wouldn't have enough time to make the next eight moves without losing on time.

Lost in thought, I was startled by a tap on my shoulder. The Dutch arbiter leaned over and said, "Mr. Kasparov, you have to write the moves." I had become so wrapped up in the game that I had forgotten to make note of the last two moves on my score sheet as required by the rules. The arbiter was of course correct to remind me of the regulations, but what a moment to be strict!

Distracted, I played my queen to the wrong square. I missed a subtlety and failed to see why a different move with the same idea would have been stronger. My move gave Karpov a clever defense, and suddenly he was one move from reclaiming his title. But under pressure from the clock, he missed the best move (though our exchange of errors would not be discovered until well after the game), and the momentum was still with me.

Karpov's best opportunity to defend had passed, and my forces surrounded the black king. I regained my sacrificed pawn with interest, and by the time we reached move forty, ending the time scramble, my position was clearly superior. The game was adjourned until the next day with the title still up in the air. It was going to be a long night.

Keeping a Grip on the Title

Getting a good night's sleep before the game had been wise, but now there was work to do. Thirteen pieces were still on the board, including queens, too much material for definitive endgame analysis. I had an extra pawn, but with such limited material, Karpov had definite chances of a draw. A lot of chess was still ahead. We spent the night investigating possible defensives and how to break them down. Before the game I gave my chances as fifty-fifty: fifty percent chance of a win, fifty percent chance of a draw.

The best news was that I could play this position forever, maneuvering around to provoke a mistake by my opponent. Black would be tied down on defense the entire time, and Karpov knew it. The prospect of such prolonged torture took its toll; I could see it in his eyes when he walked on the stage a few minutes after I did. His fatalistic expression told me that he had already lost the game psychologically, which boosted my confidence.

The maneuvering began. I remember being surprised when early on Karpov made a pawn push that my team and I had established as bad for black's defensive chances. Apparently Karpov and his team disagreed with our analysis, or perhaps it was a psychological error. Sometimes the hardest thing to do in a pressure situation is to allow the tension to persist. The temptation is to make a decision, any decision, even if it is an inferior choice. And Karpov's move made the position more concrete, reducing the level of uncertainty. But in my favor, his structure was now fixed, presenting me with clearer targets. Convinced of the quality of our analysis, I took Karpov's significant deviation from it as a mistake, not a potential improvement, further increasing my confidence.

After another ten moves of steady squeezing, I began to feel the win was in the bag. Karpov's pieces were pinned up against the wall, and a little more maneuvering would lead to decisive material gain. Later I heard that FIDE president Florencio Campomanes was busy calling a special meeting in another room to decide how to handle the closing ceremony, which was scheduled to be held on the same day. But it still looked as if this game could last forever; what was to be done? Two crises were averted at once when someone ran into the meeting room to announce, "Karpov resigned!"

It was without question the loudest and longest standing ovation I had ever received outside my native country. The theater thundered as Spanish television cut from *fútbol* to broadcast the conclusion of the match. I had done what Karpov had failed to do in 1985: won the final game and drawn the match to retain my title. This time I would have a good, long time to enjoy it.

I left the Seville stage and jumped into the arms of one of my team members, shouting, "Three years! I have three years!" Sadly, time does not stop at these moments, no matter how much we might wish it to. Those three years passed faster than I could have imagined until we were there again, Karpov and I, face-to-face in our fifth straight world championship match. Our epic duels have formed a part of chess history that most of today's top players grew up watching.

By the end of that last match in 1990—yet another narrow win for me—our career scores against each other were close. And yet in every encounter, in each match—Moscow, St. Petersburg, Seville, Lyon—at each decisive moment, I had won. This means more to me than any statistic about wins and losses. It means I performed my best when it mattered most.

ENDGAME

The Fight in Russia Today

On March 10, 2005, I played my last professional game of chess. Thirty years after I played my first major event at the national level, nearly twenty years after I became world champion, I retired at the age of forty-one. I left after winning my final tournament in my beloved Linares and still as the top-ranked player in the game, inevitably leading to numerous "Why?" inquiries from all quarters.

Faithful to my own preaching, I had looked deeply at this critical move. This was not a spontaneous move but a logical step. My shift to becoming a full-time member of the Russian political opposition movement reflected both the needs of my country and my desire to make a difference in the world around me. I was fortunate to have attained most of the ambitious goals I had set for myself in the chess world. New challenges and new ways to make an impact were waiting for me in politics and, I hoped, in writing.

One of the constant themes of this book has been how essential it is to continually challenge ourselves. The only way to develop is to venture into the unknown, to take risks, and to learn new things. We must force ourselves out of our comfort zone and trust our ability to adapt and thrive. Everything that I have written here led me to retire from the chess world. I craved new challenges and wanted to be where I felt I was wanted and needed. In fighting for the survival of Russia's fragile democracy, I found a precious cause, a worthy challenge, and a new way to channel my energy.

This decision was not about running for higher office, nor was it a personal vendetta against Vladimir Putin or anyone else. Mine is a mission of positive change. Putin is only the current symbol of what we are fighting against. I don't want my ten-year-old son to worry about Russian military service in an illegal war such as Chechnya or to fear the repression of a dictatorship. I want to have a chance to offer my vision, strategic thought, and fighting spirit to prevent those things from happening.

Many go on to ask about the dangers of opposing this Kremlin regime and if this is a foolhardy move. After all, having his father attacked or jailed won't be of much benefit to my son. To this I can only say that some things must simply be done. Succeed or fail, this is a fight that must be fought. As the Soviet dissidents famously put it, "Do what you must and so be it." Millions like me in Russia want a free press, the rule of law, social justice, and free and fair elections. My new job is to fight for those people and to fight for those fundamental rights.

To achieve these ends my colleagues and I have formed a broad nonideological coalition of true opposition groups and activists. I am working inside Russia and abroad to bring attention to the decimation of Russia's democratic institutions. My chess fame and the skills I developed in the chess world have proven equally vital to this task. My hope is that in this book I have managed to pass along some of the wisdom and strategies I've learned, and that you too will find ways to use the world's greatest game to your every advantage.

Your Life Is Your Preparation

What we make of the future is defined by how well we understand and make use of our past. Our past creates a map not only of where we have come from, but of where we are going; on it are marked the things we have valued, and the places we have found success or failure. But the most wondrous thing about this map is that vast portions of it are yet to be filled in. With insight and effort we can trace new routes to our own satisfaction.

The next part of my life will contain many new challenges. I have new goals, new people in my life, and I have left behind the only vocation I have ever known. And yet as foreign as this new course seemed at first, my life in chess has left me well prepared. I ask myself, how can I be afraid of a mere KGB lieutenant colonel after overcoming an Olympus of chess champions! Why should my nerves fail me in front of heads of state or CEOs of multinational corporations when I have spent my entire life onstage?

After a lifetime of preparation and self-examination I believe I have the tools I need to adapt to this new struggle. There are new strategies, new tactics, and I don't expect the transition to always be smooth. My personal map is full of gray areas, and its outer borders are never entirely complete. Most important, I have learned not to fear those unknown territories.

My ten-year-old son, Vadim, is reaching the age where my own childhood memories are vivid. While his life will of course be very different from mine, I dearly hope to provide him the guidance I know my father would have continued to provide me. After a hectic life I was fortunate to meet Dasha, now my friend, supporter, and wife. Above all, I'm infinitely grateful that the same person who guided me through my first career, my mother, Klara, is again with me at the start of my second. Whenever I'm faced with a difficult path, her words inspire me: "If not you, who else?"

No More Secrets

The purpose of this book is to inspire fellow explorers. We can all look at our personal maps and cast off for unknown domains where we will encounter new challenges. We can accept that failure is a necessary part of success. The faith that led Magellan to attempt to circumnavigate the globe in 1519 is why we remember him. But few remember that he was not among the eighteen survivors who completed the journey.

Like any explorer we must first plan our route, our strategy. Then we must marshal our resources, allocating them carefully while obtaining what we need and discarding any excess. Once under way, we need to maintain a sharp tactical eye by never backing away from conflict unless we are certain it best suits our needs to do so. Remaining alert for dangers and opportunities should not be allowed to distract us from our course. We must at all times be aware of changes in our environment, looking for chances to make positive exchanges that will take advantage of new conditions.

Above all, we must be conscious of every decision we make. Not only in evaluating each future course of action but in looking back to analyze our past choices and the effectiveness of the process by which we made them.

Instead of making us weary, our explorations should energize us, suffusing us with new confidence and inspiration. Our senses are sharpened, and unknown challenges soon become a sight more welcome than a familiar routine. New stimuli develop our intuition. We see the trends forming, the big picture and the details stay in focus at the same time, the dots become easier to connect. When a crisis comes, our instincts serve as an early-warning system. If we are caught by surprise, our reflexes give us the chance to take the offensive instead of playing defense.

Nearly twenty years ago I concluded a precocious autobiography with these words: "Time after time, as I've outgrown another problem or defeated another opponent, I have seen that the main battles are yet to come . . . My fight is open-ended." Now I know this fight wasn't only with the Soviet Sports Committee or FIDE or the Kremlin, but also with my own abilities and limitations. Our energies can be directed toward taking responsibility for our fates, toward creating change and making a difference. How success is measured is different for each of us. The first and most important step is realizing that the secret of success is inside.

EPILOGUE

A Strategy for Democracy

At the end of 2006, as this book was headed to the printer in several countries, the internal political chaos in Russia spilled out into the world's headlines. A British national, KGB agent defector, and harsh critic of the Kremlin, Alexander Litvinenko, was assassinated with the rare radioactive substance polonium 210. The investigation into his death currently spans at least three countries.

Litvinenko's murder came on the heels of the Moscow killing of the well-known investigative journalist Anna Politkovskaya—on Russian president Vladimir Putin's birthday no less. The killings have turned a spotlight on what the West had assumed was the autocratic-but-stable Putin regime. Suddenly the foreign media is realizing what we in the Russian opposition have been saying for years—the Kremlin is ever closer to dictatorship than democracy and yet is not stable at all.

This interest has led to a corresponding increase in attention to my own role in the opposition movement and to questions about how my former career as a chess champion has aided my mission. With that in mind, my publisher wondered if it would be appropriate to include some last-minute comments about how I have applied the lessons presented in this book to my political fight in Russia.

But this epilogue is more than a topical convenience. While writing this book and preparing my business lectures, I have discovered a great deal about synthesizing these lessons and using them in practice. It is quite accurate to say that I have been learning from my own book, confirming the old adage that the best way to learn a topic is to teach it.

The most important, and most difficult, element on my new political agenda was developing a strategy that would pump life into the anti-Putin forces. It was like sitting down to a chess game already in progress and discovering my side was close to checkmate in every variation. I could immediately draw a parallel to my first world championship match, the 1984–85 marathon against Anatoly Karpov. There I spent months a step away from total disaster, a situation that required an entirely new strategy, one based more on survival than triumph. I did it; I survived to fight another day, and the next time we met I was victorious.

The anti-Kremlin forces were in a similarly dire state in 2004. Unfortunately, in this game our opponents change the rules regularly and always to their advantage. But even in this unpredictable and unfair contest a good strategy gives us a fighting chance. I started with the fundamentals of planning: a thorough evaluation of the position and the determination of its most vital elements. Finding the outlines of the big picture came first. It was necessary to sort out allies from enemies, an easy enough task in the black-and-white world of the chessboard but far more complex in the gray realm of politics.

Two things eventually became clear to me. First, that the continued existence of organized opposition to Putin's crackdown was in no way guaranteed. We needed to dig in to survive or risk being pushed completely off the board. There is no losing with grace or reaching a peaceful accord with such an opponent. When facing an authoritarian regime bent on total control, every day you endure sends out a message of hope: "We're still here." With no access to television and other state-controlled media, it was essential for us to find other ways to get out those vital words.

Second was the need to form a coalition. The opposition was in disarray, small political and nongovernmental groups each with its own issues with the government. Despite the numerous causes and ideologies represented, I became convinced that we needed to unite, to find common cause again the repression. The one thing we all had in common was the knowledge that democracy was our only salvation. Liberals, Communists, human rights activists—we all believed, and continue to believe, that given a choice in a fair election the Russian people will reject Putin's attempt to turn our country back into a police state.

This move did not arise spontaneously. My first steps were as the cofounder and chairman of the Committee 2008: Free Choice in January 2004. This was a coalition of like-minded liberals and members of the media—that is, not just politicians—dedicated to ensuring free and fair elections in 2008, when Putin's second, and constitutionally final, term of office ends. My work there convinced me that Russia's problems were too big to solve from any internal or ideological stance.

In this book I discuss the tendency to discover problems that cannot be solved from within the available framework, and here was such a problem. Negotiations were used to gain political capital that was traded for superficial concessions by the Kremlin, a process that only perpetuated the corrupt system and made us a part of it. To have a real impact it was necessary to focus on the core issue: you were either working with the Kremlin or dedicated to dismantling the regime.

Similar ideas about uniting were already in the air, and they led to the formation of the All-Russia Civil Congress in December 2004, and I was elected cochair. I had been observing the dissatisfaction of the activists on every side. They were tired of dancing to Putin's tune while watching their party leaders cut deals for paltry handouts. The Civil

Congress was conceived as a unifying platform, but it fell short when forces from both sides of the political spectrum were as of yet unable to leave behind the Yeltsin-era civil war mentality and to work alongside their traditional adversaries. My greatest contribution would be to help bridge this gap.

In March 2005 I retired from professional chess and could plan my next tactical maneuver on the political front. A major obstacle was that the ruling administration controlled all access to television. Without access, the political grass roots were dying out all over the country. We needed to find a way to reach out beyond the Garden Ring, the wealthy center of Moscow. We needed an organization that would unify the opposition groups across the ideological divides as well as develop our nationwide network of activists. This new organization was the United Civil Front (UCF), and under this banner I traveled Russia from Vladivostok to Kaliningrad to spread our message, to talk about why the countryside was so poor and the elites so rich. And, most important, to say that it was not too late to come together and fight for our civil liberties and democracy, because only those things would improve the deteriorating standard of living.

This mixing of opposition groups has also had several positive side effects. The leftists and those still mourning the Soviet Union have come to recognize the importance of liberal democracy and political freedom. The liberals have learned to accept the need for the social programs touted by the left. Unity has not only stiffened the opposition to the Putin government, but has also clarified and advanced the specific goals of our member groups.

Each of these entities contributed to my education. I was learning quickly and we were making progress, but we still needed to reach a larger audience both inside and outside Russia. It was time to go on the offensive. The Group of Eight (seven by my count!) held a summit in St. Petersburg in the summer of 2006, and the leaders and media of the free world would be in Russia. It provided a golden opportunity to unite and also to get our message out.

We organized a convention in Moscow, an international conference that brought activists from all over Russia to share ideas and support. We also invited the international media and speakers from all over the world who were not afraid to speak strongly for democracy in the shadow of the Kremlin. My All-Russia Civil Congress cochairs and I wrote countless letters of invitation, calling in favors and twisting arms when necessary. Eventually many prominent figures contributed statements of support, although few G-8 administrations had the courage to openly endorse us. We titled our event the Other Russia Conference, so named to tell the world that the stable, democratic Russia Putin presented was not reality.

We knew we had achieved significant progress when the administration made efforts to harass us at every turn. (If this is truly a measure of success, I should be proud that the humble UCF offices were raided by security forces this month, a few days prior to our December 16 march in Moscow.) The Other Russia movement has united the Russian opposition, and although our situation is still precarious, we have succeeded in forcefully promoting ourselves into an important piece on the political chessboard.

The development of the Russian opposition has occurred in parallel with my own evolution as a political thinker. The United Civil Front added political clout to the concept of the All-Russia Civil Congress. It all finally came together, literally and figuratively, in the Other Russia.

As unfavorable as our position may still be, my evaluation of our opponents' forces discovered that they are not without their own weaknesses. Unlike the old Soviet regime, this ruling elite has a great deal at stake outside Russia. Their fortunes are in banks, stock markets, real estate, and football teams, predominantly foreign. This means they are vulnerable to external pressure. They literally cannot afford the cutting of ties that would come with open hostility between an increasingly dictatorial Russia and the West.

So far, however, it has been difficult to convince the so-called leaders of the free world and the free press to bring such pressure to bear. Putin uses Russia's energy wealth as a cudgel, and Europe's leaders meekly fall in line. Thus the third element of my strategy has been to expose this hypocrisy in as many editorial pages as I can reach.

This plan is not so shortsighted as to not keep in mind the potential consequences. It is essential to maintain our coalition because if the increasingly shaky Putin regime collapses due to internal conflict, it could lead to total chaos. It is worth remembering that just fifteen years ago the mighty Soviet regime disintegrated, much to the surprise of Western intelligence agencies. We have to always look ahead enough moves to be well prepared, even for victory!

GLOSSARY

This glossary is intended as a concise guide to some of the chess terminology used in the text. Many of the terms represent concepts explained in detail in the book.

Below is a chess diagram of the starting position. The chessboard has sixty-four squares. Each player begins with eight pieces and eight pawns.

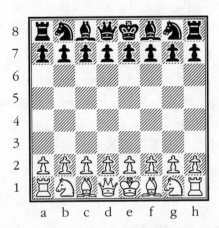

The coordinates on the edge of the board are the basis of algebraic chess notation, the symbolic language for transcribing the moves of a game. For example, "1.e4" represents a pawn moving to the e4 square on the first move. The opening moves "1.e4 e5 2.Bc4" puts a white pawn on e4, then a black pawn on e5, and then a white bishop on c4. In similar fashion games have been preserved for hundreds of years. Modern computer databases contain millions of games.

blitz chess—Games with little time given to each player, usually five minutes.

center—The four central squares of the chessboard (d4, e4, d5, e5, in algebraic notation). Controlling the center is one of the primary strategic goals. The player with control of the middle of the board has an advantage in piece mobility and, therefore, attacking potential. The positional value of various squares typically correlates to their proximity to the center.

check—When a player's king is under attack. The player in check must do one of three things: move the king, capture the attacking piece, or interpose a piece to block the line of attack.

checkmate—A position in which the king cannot avoid capture. (The king is never actually captured.) The decisive end of the game.

chess clock—A dual-action timepiece that records the amount of time each player has remaining. A player makes his move and presses the clock. This stops his clock's movement and simultaneously starts his opponent's clock. Clock time is measured for the entire game, not per move. A player loses when his time expires.

classical chess—Games with a large amount of clock time for each player. At least ninety minutes, often over two hours.

color—The pieces are referred to as white or black regardless of the actual color of the chessmen. White always moves first, which confers a substantial advantage at the professional level.

combination—A forcing sequence of moves, often sacrificial, with a specific goal.

draw—The end of a game without a decisive result. Usually this occurs by offer and acceptance between the players. It can also come about by rule in the cases of stalemate, lack of progress (fifty-move rule), or three-fold repetition of the same position. In the traditional scoring system a draw is worth half a point for each player.

endgame—The final phase of the game, coming after the middle game. Most of the pieces have been exchanged, and play becomes technical instead of strategic.

FIDE—The international chess federation, known by its French acronym (Fédération Internationale des Échecs).

gambit—An opening in which one side offers to give up material in exchange for positional advantage.

game—A single encounter between two players.

Grandmaster—The highest international title. With rare exceptions the title is awarded to a player who has achieved three qualifying tournament results and has reached a minimum 2500 rating. The Russian czar Nicholas II invented the title for the five finalists of the great 1914 tournament he sponsored in St. Petersburg. There are roughly one thousand Grandmasters in the world today. With so many "GMs," unofficial titles such as *super Grandmaster* are used to distinguish the top players.

initiative—The ability to generate threats against your opponent's position. The player with the initiative controls the course of the game through his ability to make more effective threats.

match—A series of games between two players.

material—All of the pieces and pawns on the board, minus the kings, which never leave the board. A material advantage means having the greater total value of pieces.

middle game—The phase of the game that follows the opening and precedes the endgame. The demarcation is not exact or universally agreed on. At a minimum, piece development has been completed and complex strategic and tactical play is still possible.

opening—The initial phase of the game. The opening moves are often composed of specific memorized sequences called openings. The opening is generally considered over when the pieces are no longer on their original squares and original play has begun.

pawn—The chessman of lowest value due to its limited mobility. Each side starts with eight pawns. Pawns are not usually referred to as pieces, a term used for the rest of the army. Pawns have the unique ability to promote into a piece—almost always a queen—when they reach the other side of the board.

piece values—The relative power of the chess pieces is typically measured by their value compared to a number of pawns. Knights and bishops are worth three pawns (or bishops a fraction more), rooks five pawns, the queen nine pawns.

rapid chess—Games with a short amount of clock time for each player, between blitz chess and classical chess. Typically around thirty minutes.

rating (or *Elo rating*)—A numerical representation of a player's performance based on the results of games. This rating system, developed by the American physics professor Arpad Elo, was adopted by FIDE in 1970. Grandmasters are typically rated 2500–2800+. A strong amateur tournament player might be rated 1800. An adult beginner could be expected to reach a 1200 rating in a few months of tournament play. A range of 200 points is considered a class.

sacrifice—Giving up material for positional or tactical advantage. Typically a sacrifice has a specific tactical goal, such as creating attacking chances against the opponent's king.

space—An element of a chess position representing piece mobility and the number of squares controlled. A player with an advantage in space can more freely maneuver his pieces.

tactics—The means of effecting a strategic plan. Every move in a chess game has some tactical components. Tactics require calculation and are the foundation of combinations.

time control—The amount of clock time given to the players. This is decided by rules of the tournament and varies widely, from blitz games that last ten minutes to classical games that can last seven hours.

win—A win is worth one point and occurs by checkmate or when one player resigns. Few professional games end in checkmate as players resign as soon as a loss appears inevitable.

ACKNOWLEDGMENTS

This book represents the accumulated experiences of a lifetime, but as space precludes my thanking everyone I have ever met, I will limit myself to a few people without whose help this book would not be what it is.

Owen Williams, my agent of eleven years, seeded the idea of the book and was a guiding hand in the project from a difficult opening to a winning endgame. His wife, Rebecca Williams, was the first and most devoted reader and critic of the ever-evolving manuscript. Mark Bicknell of Everyman, publisher of the My Great Predecessors book series, opened the doors to PFD, the international literary agency. Mark Reiter of PFD USA kicked the project into gear. Emily Loose, then at Penguin, moved everything in the right direction. Klaus Stadler, at my German publisher, Piper, deserves many thanks for his enthusiastic support of the book at a crucial stage.

Eduard Eilazian originated the notion of my business speeches and some of his ideas have carried through to the book. My friend and collaborator Mig Greengard has become my voice in English to the point that sometimes our writing expresses my thoughts better than my own writing in Russian! My editor Annik LaFarge at Bloomsbury championed the project from the start and tirelessly shaped the U.S. edition.

For the English translation of lines from Pushkin's *Eugene Onegin*, I used the Penguin edition, translated by Charles Johnston.

I thank Stanley Druckenmiller for his counsel as well as his steady support of chess education in the United States via the Kasparov Chess Foundation, and my friend and coach Michael Khodarkovsky (mere co-incidence!), head of the KCF. Dan and Anna Benton have helped in too many ways to count. Carl Gershman for his support of a new strategic concept for the Russian opposition. Frederic Friedel for his lasting friendship and expertise. Jim and Carol McKay for their friendship and moral support.

This book would not have been possible, indeed nothing would be possible, without the love and support of my wife, Dasha Kasparova. She was an indispensable anchor during my difficult transition away from professional chess and she is just as indispensable now.

INDEX

A NOTE ON THE AUTHOR

Garry Kasparov grew up in Baku, Azerbaijan (USSR), and became the youngest-ever world chess champion in 1985. He held the world title until 2000. He retired from professional chess in March 2005 to found the United Civil Front in Russia and has dedicated himself to establishing free and fair elections in his homeland. A regular contributor to the *Wall Street Journal* editorial page, Kasparov travels around the world to address corporations and business audiences on strategy and leadership, and he appears frequently in the international media to talk about both chess and politics. When not traveling, he divides his time between Moscow and St. Petersburg.